HEATHROW

2000 YEARS OF HISTORY

SECOND EDITION

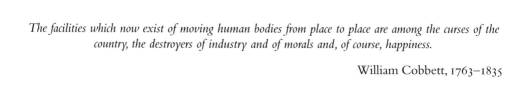

The facilities which now exist of moving human bodies from place to place are among the curses of the country, the destroyers of industry and of morals and, of course, happiness.

William Cobbett, 1763–1835

HEATHROW

2000 YEARS OF HISTORY

SECOND EDITION

PHILIP SHERWOOD

The
History
Press

Philip Sherwood is a retired chemist turned local historian who as a Principal Scientific Officer in the Scientific Civil Service has worked for the Transport (formerly Road) Research Laboratory and the Royal Commission on Environmental Pollution. He is a Fellow of the Royal Society of Chemistry, an active member of several amenity and environmental groups, the Publications Editor of the Hayes and Harlington Local History Society and represents the London Branch of the Campaign for the Protection of Rural England on the CPRE Aviation Advisory Group. In addition to several technical publications and this edition he has compiled several previous publications in the 'Britain in Old Photographs' series.

First published in 1990 as *The History of Heathrow*
First published under this title in 1999
Reprinted in 2001

This edition first published in 2009
The History Press
The Mill, Brimscombe Port
Stroud, Gloucestershire, GL5 2QG
www.thehistorypress.co.uk

Reprinted 2011, 2012

British Library Cataloguing in Publication Data.
A catalogue record for this book is available from the British Library.

ISBN 978 0 7524 5086 2

Printed and bound in Great Britain by
Marston Book Services Limited, Didcot

Contents

Acknowledgements

Many of the photographs reproduced in the text come from my own private collection accumulated over many years. They include some that have always belonged to me and others given to me, from time to time, by people with their own reminiscences of pre-airport Heathrow. In particular mention should be made of members of old farming families, such as the Wilds, Philps and Heywards who farmed in the area and the late John Chinery who had an extensive collection of material relating to the Fairey Aviation Company. Other individuals who have donated valuable material include the late Josh Marshall, Ken Pearce, Douglas Rust, Graham Smeed and John Walters. Organisations whose material has been used with permission include The National Archives (TNA), Hillingdon Borough Libraries, the West Drayton Local History Society (WDLHS), the Hayes and Harlington Local History Society (HHLHS), the Uxbridge Gazette and BAA plc. Acknowledgements to these organisations for reproducing their photographs are given, where appropriate, within the text. In the case of living persons who have donated material, their contribution is also acknowledged in the appropriate place. Copies of the maps originating from The National Archives are based on Crown copyright material and are reproduced by permission of the Controller of Her Majesty's Stationery Office.

Apologies are offered to anyone whose material has been inadvertently used without acknowledgement.

Foreword

In the eleven years that have elapsed since I wrote the foreword to the first edition, which is reproduced below, all the gloomy predictions that were then made about the further development of Heathrow have proven to be all too true. Permission to construct a Fifth Terminal at Heathrow was granted subject to certain conditions that were soon relaxed. So not surprisingly, and despite all assurances made at the time of the T5 Inquiry, pressure has since grown for the construction of a third E–W runway accompanied by a sixth terminal. Nor has it stopped there as British Airways is already talking about a fourth runway and a seventh terminal to be constructed by 2030!

The first edition is therefore so badly out-dated that it was considered opportune to prepare a new edition to take accounts of developments that have occurred since it was published and to consider what may happen in the years that lay ahead. That part of the first edition that dealt with the history of the area before 1944 is reproduced virtually unchanged with only minor editorial amendments. The same is substantially true of the accounts that describe how the airport was conceived and its development up to 1990. However, so much has happened since then and so much is predicted to occur in the foreseeable future that an entirely new section has been written to take account of this. The Foreword to the first edition concluded with the view that 'as a Society we will need to pay a higher price for air travel to offset the unacceptable disturbance that is caused by the civil aviation industry. Until such time is reached it will never prove possible to write a history of Heathrow that will remain up-to-date for very long.'

This remains the case but events outside the influence of the aviation industry may well mean that it will be impossible for the growth of aviation to continue at the pace that has occurred in the past 50 years. Not least is the growing concern about the effects of climate change and the increasing contribution of aviation to the concentration of carbon dioxide in the atmosphere. All informed scientific opinion takes the view that the dramatic increase in carbon dioxide in the atmosphere is almost certainly the cause of global warming and it would be incredibly foolish not to act accordingly. However, it would seem that the aviation industry is more concerned to increase its profits rather than to worry about an environmental catastrophe in the years to come. The views of the industry on this subject can be likened to that of the tobacco industry which for long denied that there was any link between smoking and health and went so far as to fund research to 'prove' that smoking was not a health hazard.

P.T. Sherwood
Harlington 2009

Foreword to the First Edition

There are many accounts of Heathrow, mostly written by civil aviation enthusiasts. These, together with the self-congratulatory propaganda of BAA and British Airways, mean that the civil aviation aspect of Heathrow is well-covered and yet another book on this subject would be superfluous. Less well known is the long history of the Heathrow area which is quite separate from the airport. Nor is the effect that the growth of the airport has had on the once pleasant and peaceful countryside of West Middlesex, which has been destroyed in less than 50 years, ever considered. The book therefore concentrates on these aspects. The change from a relatively prosperous, largely agricultural, area to the world's busiest international airport is often referred to as progress – a word which the dictionary defines as, 'an advance to something better or later in development'. Anybody who can remember what the Heathrow area was like before the advent of the airport will surely agree that progress is hardly the appropriate word.

The development of the airport has totally changed the social structure of the communities living around it. Many of these now depend on the airport for their economic well-being and resent any criticism of it. However, as relative newcomers they should accept that there are those who are even more resentful of the manner in which the airport came about. They are, in any case, outnumbered by those who live within earshot of Heathrow who derive no benefit from it but are reminded every minute of the day of its presence. Ever since the airport was established the rights of people have been subordinated to the interests of civil aviation to the point where one could say of Heathrow as Goldsmith wrote in his poem 'The Deserted Village' – '*Ill fares the land to hast'ning ills a prey, where wealth accumulates and men decay.*'

The fact that Heathrow plays a vital role in the national economy cannot be questioned, but the major British airport would be bound to play such a role wherever it was situated. The argument against Heathrow as the site for the major airport is that it was singularly ill-chosen and the development should not have taken place by what was little short of fraud. The claim has always been made that Heathrow was developed as a result of an urgent war-time need for the RAF to have a bomber base in the London area. Research among the Air Ministry files in the Public Record Office shows that there was never such a need and the airfield was developed from the start as a civil airport for London. The War Cabinet was deceived into giving approval for the development, even although it meant diverting resources away from the war-effort when preparations were being made for the Normandy landings. The Defence of the Realm Act 1939 was used by the Air Ministry to requisition the land and to circumvent the public inquiry that would otherwise have had to be held. The book describes the results of the examination of the files that show the true story behind the development.

   ⋆ Elated with its success of establishing the airport by 'fraudulent' means during the latter part of WWII the civil aviation lobby has continued ever since to seek to expand the airport boundaries. The attempt to build a fifth terminal is only the latest of these plans. Each proposed expansion is claimed at the time to be the last but once permission is given it inevitably leads to further demands. The fourth terminal, which BAA claimed to be its last ever demand, was followed within three years of its opening by an application to build a fifth terminal! No doubt, if this were to be permitted, it would inevitably be followed by a demand for additional runway capacity which in turn would be followed by proposals for a sixth terminal.

The philosophy of 'predict and provide' has belatedly been abandoned in road building as it has become increasingly apparent that the predictions are largely self-fulfilling – traffic grows to fill the space available. The same is equally true of air transport and it is to be hoped that it will eventually be realised that we cannot simply go on extrapolating ever-rising forecasts of growth in air traffic indefinitely into the future without unacceptable environmental consequences. In the words of Michael Heseltine, when Secretary of State for the Environment (1992), *'We have now reached the point where we cannot always respond to demands for either development or transport infrastructure simply because those demands exist.'*

As a Society we will need to pay a higher price for air travel to offset the unacceptable disturbance that is caused by the civil aviation industry. Until such time is reached it will never prove possible to write a history of Heathrow that will remain up-to-date for very long.

★ Subsequent events have shown that these predictions proved to be all too true!

PART ONE

Heathrow Before the Airport

Chapter One

The Geographical Background

The Landscape

South Middlesex consists of a series of flat gravel terraces – the Flood Plain Terrace gravel roughly 25 feet above sea level, the Taplow Terrace at roughly 50 feet and the Boyn Hill at roughly 100 feet. The gravel of the last is rather coarse and apt to be sterile but the other two usually have a covering of brickearth.

Heathrow is in a part of the Thames valley in which over the course of several million years the Thames has gradually moved southwards. During periods of glaciation followed by subsequent thaw the river must have been flowing at such a speed that it was able to carry gravels from the glaciers and icefields to the north and west. Fast flowing water can carry clay and silt much more easily than gravel so that when the flow rate decreased, as the river approached the sea, the gravel would have been deposited first. As the sea level rose with the melting of the ice the flow rate decreased still further and allowed the clay and silt to settle out on top of the gravel previously deposited. This layer dried out as the river retreated to give the brickearth deposits which overlie the gravel in many parts of the Thames valley. The fact that the gravel and the overlaying soils were deposited under water means that the land is flat and level in character with a general slope of no more than ten feet per mile

The general flatness of the area, which can be seen in the previous photograph, is its most notable characteristic leading to unkind references not altogether deserved. For example the 'Beauties of England and Wales,' published in the early 19th century, describes the area thus 'The whole of the (Harmondsworth) parochial district has an undesirable flatness of surface and is intersected by small rivers or streams which creep in dull obscurity without imparting to any spot an attractive portion of the picturesque.'

Heathrow from the air, 1935 (Photograph courtesy of Quadrant/Flight International). This view is to the north-east with the hangar of the Fairey aerodrome (see page 62) almost in the centre. It gives a good impression of the rural nature of the area at this time with all the land in intensive cultivation. The road running from the bottom right-hand corner is High Tree Lane which crosses the Duke of Northumberland's River and then joins Heathrow Road turning left towards Perry Oaks and right to loop round to join the Bath Road at the 'Three Magpies' (see page 43).

Geography

Historically the Heathrow area occupies the south-east corner of Harmondsworth parish with the Bath Road forming a convenient boundary between it and the rest of the parish. The villages to the north pre-date the Bath Road and when established their centres would have been surrounded on all four sides by their open fields on the fertile brickearth with their common land to the south of the brickearth and on the less fertile Taplow Terrace gravels On the geological map the Bath Road which was established long after the villages can thus be seen to follow the boundary between these two geological formations. This does not mean that there is an abrupt change at this boundary but the thickness of the brickearth overlaying the gravel (which can be many feet in thickness to the north of the Bath Road) becomes gradually reduced in a southerly and easterly direction. Towards the extreme south-east of the parish the soil covering is very thin and was part of Hounslow Heath, which had a soil described by Cobbett in his 'Rural Rides' (1830) as 'a nasty strong dirt upon a bed of gravel and is a sample of all that is bad and villainous in look.' For good measure Cobbett considered that the labouring people of this area 'looked to be about half Saint Giles's, dirty and had every appearance of drinking gin.'

The Twin Rivers

Two rivers skirt the western and southern boundaries of the airport, both are man-made. One was constructed to supply water to the mills at Isleworth, the other to provide water to Hampton Court.

Rocque's Map of Middlesex, 1754.
This is the earliest known large-scale (2 miles to the inch) map of the area. The Bath Road runs east-west across the middle of the map with Harmondsworth, Sipson and Harlington to its north and Heathrow to the south. Rocque gives the name as Heath Row but nearly all other sources of information, before and since, give it as

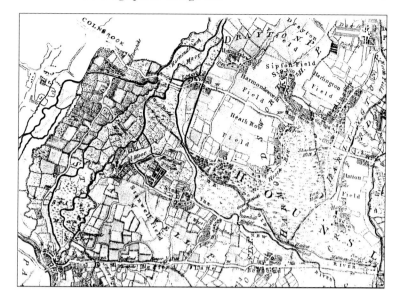

one word. Heathrow is shown as being on the edge of Hounslow Heath forming part of the common land of Harmondsworth Parish and to the west of Heathrow Road is Heathrow Field, one of the pre-Inclosure open arable fields of Harmondsworth Parish. Comparison of Rocque's map with the Harmondsworth Inclosure map shows that, apart from the Bath Road and Heathrow Road, most of the roads in the area were re-aligned at the time of the Inclosure. In the otherwise flat landscape, Rocque defines two areas close to the Harmondsworth/Harlington parish boundary as Shasbury Hill and Fern Hill.

Harmondsworth Parish before Inclosure (From VCH Middlesex Vol.4). This map combines the information in Rocque's map and the Harmondsworth Inclosure map of 1819. It shows the open fields and common land of the parish and the roads as re-aligned by the Inclosure Commissioners. The southern boundary of the parish follows the course of the Duke of Northumberland's River which is marked on the

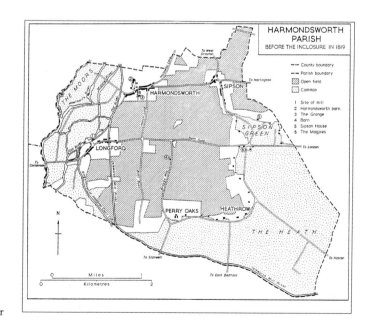

map as the Isleworth Mill River. The south-east corner of the parish formed part of Hounslow Heath and was the common land of the parish. For a map of the parish after the inclosure see page 21.

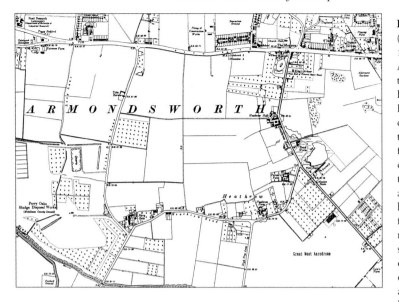

Heathrow, 1935
(From 2.5 inches –
1 mile OS Map).
A comparison of
this map with the
Harrmondsworth
Inclosure Map
on page 13 shows
that comparatively
few changes had
occurred between
the Inclosure of 1819
and 1935. The road
layout is identical, the
field pattern is still
recognisable although
some consolidation
of the holdings has
occurred and a little
additional building
has taken place. The
major change is the presence of the Fairey aerodrome but even that had little impact on the landscape (see
page 21). On this map the area of Shasbury/Schapsbury Hill is marked as 'Earthwork' in Gothic letters.

**Aerial view
of Heathrow
area, 1940.** This
photograph is one of
a series taken on 27
September 1940 by
the Luftwaffe during
the Battle of Britain.
Unfortunately
the photograph
immediately to the
south which was
taken on the same
occasion is badly
obscured by clouds.
In this photograph
Heathrow lies to the
south of the Bath
Road which crosses
the photograph
diagonally at the
bottom left-hand
corner. Towards
the top right-hand
extremity is the
uncompleted
alignment of
the Parkway at
Cranford, work on which had started in 1939 as part of the proposed extensions to Heston aerodrome
(see page 60). The Luftwaffe archives are the most complete aerial cover of Britain up to 1940. They were
captured at the end of the war and are now in the US National Archives in Washington which supplied
this photograph.

Since both of these places are situated on the River Thames it may seem strange that so much trouble should have been taken to divert water from the River Colne several mile to the west but the Thames although nearby could not be diverted to flow up-hill. The presence of both rivers at Heathrow caused problems with the original construction of the airport and later for airport extensions. Consequently both rivers have had to be diverted on more than one occasion to allow first for the construction of the airport and then for later expansion.

The Duke of Northumberland's River

This is the older of the two and is marked as the 'Old River' in Rocque's map of 1754 , the 'Isleworth Mill River' in the Harmondsworth Inclosure Map of 1819 and now known as the 'Duke of Northumberland's River' (after the owners of Syon House at Isleworth since the 17th century) . It was probably constructed in the 15th or 16th centuries to run from the Colne just to the north of Harmondsworth by way of Longford, Heathrow and Bedfont to join the Crane for a short distance at Baber Bridge before proceeding on its own course to Isleworth for the purpose of originally providing power to the manorial water mill at Isleworth on the Thames. It is probable that the river followed the line of a natural watercourse to some degree because in the Heathrow area it formed the boundary between the parishes of Harmondsworth and Stanwell which would have been established long before the river was formed. The route of its former channel continued to mark the southern boundary of Harmondsworth parish and hence of the Borough of Hillingdon until the boundary changes in 1994.

The course of the river was changed in the 1947 as a result of the construction of Heathrow Airport so that at one point it went underground and shared a channel with the Longford River.

Preparation of new course for the twin rivers, 1949. During the construction of the airport both rivers were diverted to follow a more southerly course and for a short distance they now flow side-by-side in twin channels alongside Bedfont Road, Stanwell.

Twin Rivers at Stanwell, 2007. This photograph was taken from approximately the same vantage point is the earlier one. The large house on the left is common to both photographs although in the intervening years its walls have been whitened. The view is to the west with the Duke of Northumberland's River on the right and the Longford River on the left.

Marker blocks recording the former courses of the Twin Rivers. These were placed at intervals 'in order that a permanent record of the old beds could be maintained.' Those marking the course of the D.O.N's River soon disappeared but some of those marking the course of the Longford River survived up to the time of the construction of the Fifth Terminal.

Opposite below: **Duke of Northumberland's River, Syon Park.** The river still flows serenely through the grounds of Syon House unaffected by the depredations further upstream. The lake shown here was created from the river by Capability Brown in the mid 18th century.

Twin Rivers Diversion, 2004 (D. McCartney). The construction of the Fifth Terminal meant that an additional 3.5 km length of the D.O.N. River had to be diverted westwards together with a 2.5 km section of the Longford River. The photograph above shows the diverted twin rivers looking north from the T5 Welcome Roundabout, Heathrow Airport, 14th May 2004 soon after the completion of the diversions. The Longford River is on the right and the Duke of Northumberland's River is on the left. The photograph below shows that some attempt was made to recreate the appearance of the river banks but it contrasts badly with previous scenes. In any case it has since been completely negated by the need to cover the rivers with netting to prevent water birds from using the rivers because they might pose a hazard to aircraft.

The Long Water, Hampton Court. The Longford River provides all the water features in the grounds of Hampton Court and the adjoining Bushey Park.

The course of the river has been altered again to allow for the construction of Heathrow Airport's Terminal 5. In a project known as the 'Twin Rivers Diversion Scheme', both the Longford River and the Duke of Northumberland's River have been put in adjoining channels running around the western perimeter of the site at ground level, no longer having to pass under the airport.

The Longford River

This was dug on the orders of Charles I who, in 1638, commissioned an inquiry into 'how the waters of the Colne could be brought over Hounslow Heath into the Park' so as to improve the water supply of Hampton Court. The name it was known by in the early 19th century 'The Hampton Court Canal' made clear its purpose, but by 1834 it had been re-named the King's River, and on the first large-scale edition of the Ordnance Survey map (published in 1868) it was called 'The Queen's or Cardinal's River'. As its name suggests it leaves the Colne at Longford just to the north of the point where the King's Bridge carries the Bath Road over the river. This bridge like the remainder of the river is still maintained by the Crown Commisioners whose consent had to be obtained before the river could be diverted.

Chapter Two

Pre-History

Heathrow appears to have been the last of the post-Roman settlements to be formed in Harmondsworth Parish. Harmondsworth itself is in the north-west of the parish and the name is first mentioned in an Anglo-Saxon charter of 780 AD when land in a place called Hermonds was granted by Offa, King of Mercia to his servant Aeldred. By the time of Domesday the name had become Hermondesworde. Sipson, now the second largest settlement in the parish, is first referred to as Subeston in a custumal of the manor of Harmondsworth dating from 1110, Longford is first mentioned in 1337 and the first known reference to Heathrow is in 1453. All the names are of Anglo-Saxon origin and in all cases must have existed long before their first recorded references.

However, long before Saxon times there were settlements in the area. No written record exists but there is plenty of archaeological evidence for human occupation (1). The most significant in the Heathrow area was the discovery during the construction of the airport of an extensive iron-age settlement.

The appearance of the area labelled either as Shasbury Hill, Schapsbury Hill or Camp on old maps such as Rocque's map of middlesex published in 1754 (see page 13) shows that it must have been a significant feature in the flat landscape. Pre-war Ordnance Survey maps show a rectangular area, either labelled 'Earthwork' as in Figure 2 or 'Camp', on the Harmondsworth side of the Harmondsworth-Harlington parish boundary and about ¼-mile south of the Bath Road. The earliest recorded reference to the site is in Camden's 'Britanniae' 1586 which says 'on the north edge of (Hounslow) Heath towards King's Arbour is a Roman camp; a simple work and not large.' It is mentioned again in the map of the Hundred of Isleworth drawn by Moses Glover in 1635. It is just beyond the boundary of Glover's map but, near to the River Crane, he records 'In this Heathe (i.e. Hounslow Heath) hath many camps bin pitched . . . whereof the forme of two yet in parte remaineth not far beyond this rive. By the name of Shakesbury Hilles.' Rocque's map of 1754 records the two 'camps', mentioned by Glover, under the names of Shasbury Hill and Fern Hill. A suggested derivation of 'Shakesbury' is that it could mean 'robber's camp' and the numerous highwaymen operating on Hounslow Heath could well have used it as a hideout.

Both were featured again in 1784 in the map prepared for General Roy showing the position of his baseline across Hounslow Heath. The maps of Rocque and Roy depict the 'camps' as rectangular enclosures of approximately equal size. Roy, while retaining the name of Fern Hill used by Rocque gives the name of the other camp as 'Schapsbury Hill'.

The Harmondsworth Inclosure map of 1819 records 'Schapsbury Hill' under the same name used by Roy but does not record Fern Hill. Cotton (2) suggests that, as its name indicates, Fern Hill had, by then, become overgrown and therefore difficult to locate on the ground. The maps indicate that both Fern Hill and Schapsbury Hill were distinctive features which must have been particularly prominent in the otherwise flat terrain.

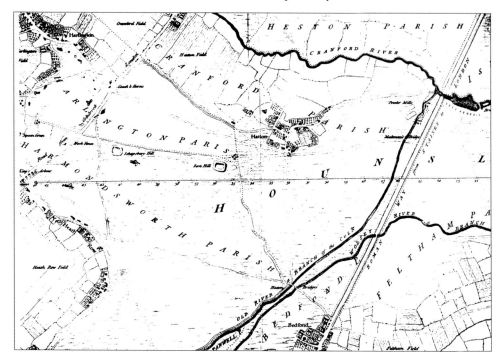

Western end of General Roy's 'Plan shewing the situation of the base measured on Hounslow Heath 1784' (see page 25). Roy's account of his survey was published in the Proceedings of the Royal Society and the map shown above is a copy of that which accompanies his account. Schapsbury Hill and Fern Hill are both clearly depicted. (The Royal Society).

Schapsbury Hill (Caesar's Camp)

The site of Schapsbury Hill was examined by Stukeley in 1723 who believed it to be a Roman encampment. He said it was nearly perfect and sixty paces square, but he did not say why he recognised it as a Roman site or why he called it 'Caesar's Camp'. Stukeley's drawing of the site is shown below.

Lysons, writing at the end of the 18th century also mentions the earthwork, stating that it consisted of a single trench about three hundred feet square. It is also mentioned in an account written soon after the Inclosure (1819) (3) which says: '*Heathrow is situated to the south of the Bath Road on the margin of Hounslow Heath. At a short distance from this place towards the east, were, until recently, the remains of an ancient camp supposed to be Roman. The vestiges were about 300 feet square and the embankment was defended by a single trench only. The parish of Harmondsworth has recently been enclosed by Act of Parliament and the plough has thrown into furrows the castramentation raised by the Romans in pride of military art.*'

However, enough survived for it to have been mentioned in the Victoria County History (4) which recorded that '*three quarters of a mile north-east of Heathrow, immediately south of the Bath Road, a small square camp about 380 feet square was extant until the autumn of 1906. It is now ploughed perfectly flat, leaving no trace.*' This last statement must have been an exaggeration since it was still significant enough for it to be marked on maps up to the time of its obliteration by the airport. The full significance of the site became apparent in 1944, when hurried excavations by Grimes (5) prior to the construction of the main runway at Heathrow revealed the true significance of the earthwork. The datable evidence showed that the enclosure went back to the dawn of the British Early Iron Age i.e. about 500 BC.

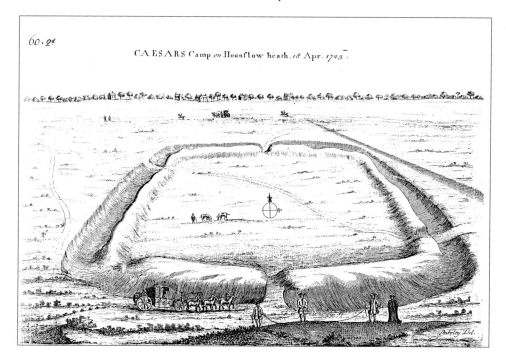

60.2ᵈ

CAESARS Camp on Hounslow heath. 18 Apr. 1723.

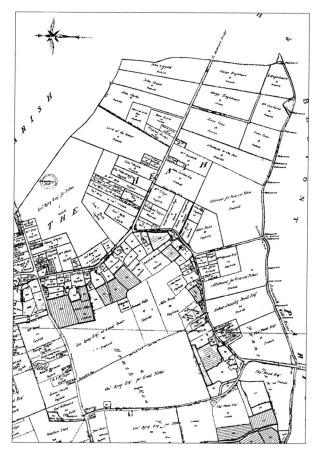

Above: **Caesar's Camp on Hounslow Heath, 1723.** The site of Schapsbury Hill as recorded in 1723 by Stukeley who believed it to be a Roman encampment. The drawing shows how well preserved the earthwork when this part of Hounslow Heath was yet to be enclosed.

SW Portion of the Harmondsworth Inclosure Map, 1819. This map is unusual in that east is shown at the top of the map; it therefore has to be turned through 90° to get the same orientation as the other maps in the book. The original was drawn to a very large-scale (18 inches to the mile) and in great detail to illustrate the re-allocation of land within the parish. It shows clearly how the open fields and the common land were split into small enclosed fields. Shasbury Hill of Rocque's map has become Schapsbury Hill but no mention is made of Fern Hill.

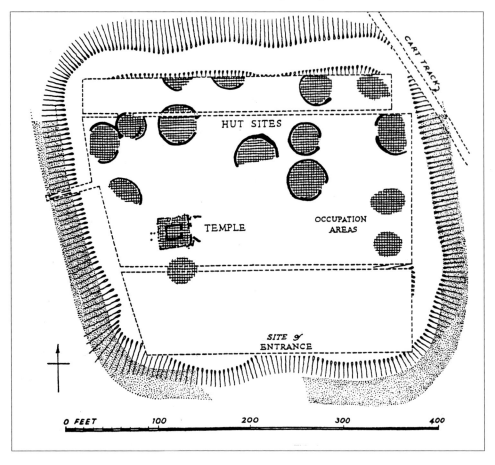

CART TRACK?

HUT SITES

OCCUPATION
AREAS

TEMPLE

SITE of
ENTRANCE

0 FEET   100   200   300   400

Simplified plan of the Heathrow site as finally excavated by Grimes in 1944 showing the distribution of the hut sites and occupation areas and the position of the temple. (From Grimes's article in 'Archaeology', Summer 1948.)

Grimes reported that, by 1944, the rampart and ditch were much spread and reduced and defied photography from the ground. The bank stood nowhere more than two feet high, its clearest indication being provided by the creep of the plough soil away from its crest, which exposed the light soil of the rampart beneath. The entrance, to the south, was barely discernible. The excavations showed that in the northern half of the enclosure had been a series of eleven huts.

This picture of a comparatively small domestic area with a large vacant space probably used as a farmyard and enclosure for cattle was in itself not particularly remarkable. However, it was no ordinary farm as the excavations along the west side near the base of the bank, were of much greater significance as they revealed the existence of a remarkable rectangular building, 37 x 32 feet in size, that could only have been a temple and of a type earlier than anything previously recorded in this country. It consisted of a central shrine, which must have had solid wooden walls. enclosed by an outer rectangle of thick wooden posts. It was probably covered by a thatched roof, that extended downwards from a central ridge-pole to the outer posts. It has been likened to a classical Greek temple with the stone columns replaced by wooden posts and the stone-walled sanctuary by a structure like a log cabin. The drawing below gives an artist's reconstruction of what the site probably looked like. This important, indeed unique, site was destroyed and buried under the main runway in 1944.

Reconstruction of Early Iron Age settlement at Heathrow (drawing by Alan Sorrell, reproduced by permission of the Museum of London). The illustration gives an artist's reconstruction of the site based on the information then available in the 1960s. Later re-appraisal of the archaeological investigations now suggests that there was a considerable amount of artistic license in this drawing.

Fern Hill

Much less is known about Fern Hill, the other earthwork recorded on early maps. Unlike Schapsbury Hill, it was not mentioned by Lysons (1800) and was omitted from the Harmondsworth Inclosure map referred to above. The earliest large-scale Ordnance Survey map (1865) of the area shows that within 50 years of the Inclosure the site had become an orchard so the earthwork would have become even less significant at ground level and not visible at all from the air. The orchard was grubbed up at the outbreak of war and an aerial photograph taken in the Summer of 1949, before the airport had encroached on to the site, shows a small circular cropmark enclosure situated at Hatton Cross. This has been identified as Fern Hill by Cotton (2) who has demonstrated that it was not, as the early maps suggest, rectangular in plan but more nearly circular with a diameter of about 250 feet. The site of the earthwork now lies partly beneath an aircraft hangar erected in the early 1950s.

Excavations at the Terminal 5 (Perry Oaks) site

When the northern runway was extended in 1969 the remains of a Neolithic segmented ditch were uncovered. It was believed that this and other ditches were probably linked with the embanked ceremonial avenue or 'cursus' monument which had been discovered on the western edge of the airport . This consisted of two substantial parallel ditches 22 yards apart which run in a straight line NNW from Stanwell, under the western edge of the airport to Bigley Ditch north of the Colnbrook by-pass. Further evidence for the existence of this cursus materialised when excavations began on the Perry Oaks site prior to the construction of the 5th Terminal. This revealed that it was 4km long with a 20 metre wide raised pathway. It dated from 3800 BC and is the second largest of its type that has been found in the UK.

The Perry Oaks excavations were one of the largest ever archaeological investigations ever to be undertaken in Great Britain. Furthermore, unlike the hurried emergency war-time excavations carried out in 1944 when construction of the airport began, there was ample time and they were well-funded. This was because of the length of the T5 planning inquiry (see Chapter 1 of Part 2) and the fact that BAA anticipated that a condition of planning consent, if granted, would involve a preliminary archaeological investigation. The resulting excavations helped to shed light on more than 8000 years of human history. Apart from the cursus among other findings were more than 80,000 artefacts dating back as far as the Mesolithic era 6,000 years ago – including 18,000 pieces of pottery, 40,000 pieces of flint and a 2,500-year-old wooden bowl – a unique find for this country. The discovery of ancient field boundaries suggested that individually owned farms sprang up around 2000BC – some 500 years earlier than previously believed.

The results of the T5 investigations have been published in a Framework Archaeology Monograph (6).

Other archaeological features

An aerial photograph of Heathrow taken in June 1941 reveals a well-defined circular cropmark just to the north of Heathrow Road and between its junction with Cains Lane and High Tree Lane. Slightly to the south-west of this is a semi-circular cropmark on the south side of, and touching, Heathrow Road; this could have been a circular enclosure cut in half by the road (which is much later and probably post-medieval) but there is no trace of it on the north side of the road. The significance of these will never be known as the site is now in the central terminal area of the airport.

References

1. Cotton, J., Mills, J. and Clegg, G, *Archaeology in West Middlesex*. Hillingdon Borough Libraries, 1986
2. Cotton, J., *St. John's Camp alias Fern Hill: A forgotten West Middlesex Landscape*. Transactions of the London and Middlesex Archaeological Society 1990, 41, 1–8
3. Anon., *The History of London and Middlesex, Volume 20*. Undated (c.1820). Possibly a late edition of Brewster and Brayley's 'Beauties of England and Wales')
4. Victoria County History, *A History of the County of Middlesex*, Volume II, 1911
5. Grimes, W.F., *A pre-historic temple at London Airport*. Archaeology 1948, 1 (1), 74–78
6. Lewis, J. et al, *Landscape Evolution in the Middle Thames Valley : Heathrow Terminal 5 Excavations*. Volume 1 was published in 2006 but as of early 2009 no further volumes have yet appeared

Chapter Three

General Roy and the Ordnance Survey

There is a little corner of Heathrow which literally helped to put everywhere else in Great Britain on the map. Tucked away off the Bath Road between Heathrow Police Station and the perimeter road is a plaque and a half-buried cannon which commemorate a major breakthrough in the history of mapmaking. Exactly 27406.19 feet to the south-east there is an identical memorial in the centre of a housing estate in Hampton. The memorials mark the ends of an invisible baseline measured out in 1784, under the supervision of Major General William Roy, across what was then part of Hounslow Heath to establish a baseline of accurately known length as a prelude to an accurate trigonometrical survey of Great Britain.

Roy chose the site, *because of its vicinity to the capital and the Royal Observatory at Greenwich, its great extent and the extraordinary levelness of the surface without any local obstructions whatever to render the measurement difficult.* One end of his baseline was at King's Arbour, Heathrow and the other at Hampton some five miles away.

There is a popular myth that King's Arbour got its name from the fact that the area was used for stabling the horses of George III who would not use inns for changing horses on his way to Windsor, but kept an establishment of his own. However, the name was in existence some 200 years before the reign of George III; a Survey of the Manor of Harmondsworth made in 1548 includes a statement that, among other things, Edward Stokewood holds *'One tenement with eight acres of land to the same lying at King's Arbour called Mayhouse Croft, late William Mayhewe.'* The name also occurs in the Court Rolls of the Manor for 18 October 1559, when tenants were ordered to make a fence 'from Kynges Arber to Thykattes Gate'.

As the name was well established in the sixteenth Century this effectively disposes of the myth that the name comes from King George having a stable there. The King referred to in the name was probably a member of the King family whose name occurs in records dating back as far as 1390 relating to Harmondsworth parish. The Harmondsworth Inclosure Award of 1819 records the King as the owner of the piece of land around the cannon at the western end of General Roy's baseline at Heathrow. This is probably the origin of the myth that the land was used by George III for stabling his horses. It was only nine perches (30¼ square yards) in area and thus rather small to be used for stabling.

Arbour may equate with the modern meaning of the word which came into English from the French. It can, however, have a much older origin derived from Old English 'earth-burh' meaning earth fort. As King's Arbour was adjacent to the earthwork mentioned in the previous section it is quite possible that in this case the Arbour refers to the earthwork.

The origin of Roy's work was in a proposal he submitted in 1763 for a comprehensive 'general survey of the whole Island at public cost'. The proposal was seriously considered but dropped on the grounds that *'it would be a work of much time and labour, and attended with great Expence to the Government.'* It was resurrected in 1783 when the Director of the Paris

Observatory submitted a paper to George III suggesting the triangulation of south-east England. This, connected to the French network, would provide a means of establishing the relative positions of the Greenwich and Paris Observatories. The paper was forwarded to Sir Joseph Banks, the President of the Royal Society, who immediately proposed that Roy should take charge of the project

The exact location of the baseline was agreed on the ground by Roy accompanied by Sir Joseph Banks and Charles Blagden. The terminals were at King's Arbour and the Poor House at Hampton; soldiers were used to clear the ground between the two points and generally assist in the survey. The spire of a church, which Roy subsequently discovered was that of Banstead in Surrey, was found to be directly in line with the two ends of the base and provided a useful sighting point.

Rough measurement of the base, using a 100 ft. steel chain, started on 16 June 1784 and was completed by the end of the month. On 15 July precise measurements began using wooden (deal) rods but the weather was bad and it soon became apparent that, because of expansion and contraction of the wood with changes in humidity, wooden rods would not be sufficiently accurate. Glass tubes (referred to by Roy as rods) were suggested as a possible alternative by one of Roy's assistants and somewhat surprisingly were found to be suitable. It proved possible to obtain glass rods about 20 ft. in length and 1 inch in diameter and these rods were mounted in wooden cases. By using specially designed equipment for handling the rods measurements could be made along the length of the baseline. Work on this started on 17 August and was completed by the end of the month. An amusing aside was Roy's complaint that the carriages passing along the 'Great Road' (the old Staines Road running from Hounslow to Staines) continually interrupted his work. The distance as measured by Roy was 27404.01 feet.

Cannon at each end of the baseline. Roy marked the terminals of the baseline by wooden pipes and waggon wheels sunk into the ground. In 1791 these were found to be in an advanced state of decay and they were replaced by two cannon. Selected from those unfit for service at Woolwich Arsenal, the guns were half-buried in the ground muzzle upwards, one at each end of the baseline. In 1926, at the suggestion of Sir Charles Close (Director General of the Ordnance Survey 1911-1922) bronze plaques were fixed to each gun to commemorate the 200th anniversary of Roy's birth. The photograph on the left shows the cannon at King's Arbour, Heathrow just before its removal in 1944. Unlike its twin, the cannon in the photograph on the right at the south-east terminal of the baseline at Hampton has never been removed. When installed in 1791 it stood in open country near the Hampton Poor House but it is now stands in Cannon Close which is a turning off Roy Grove and is surrounded by a small housing estate. (Left photograph: S. Heyward; right: G. Smeed.)

Removal of the cannon at Heathrow, 1944 (M.Heyward). When construction of the airport started in 1944 the cannon at Heathrow was removed for safekeeping and taken to the Headquarters of the Ordnance Survey then at Chessington.

Unveiling memorial to General Roy 1967 (G. Smeed). In 1967 it was realised that something tangible should be done at Heathrow to commemorate Roy's achievement. This took the form of placing a plaque on the wall of Heathrow Police Station which stands due north of the original site of the cannon. This photograph shows the plaque being unveiled by General R.C.A. Edge, the Director of the Ordnance Survey on 17 November 1967.

Return of the cannon 1968. Because it was thought to be a potential danger to aircraft taxiing along a proposed runway, the cannon was removed in August 1944 and stored at the Ordnance Survey temporary headquarters at Chessington. The cannon was returned to Heathrow in 1968 and remained in the Engineering Department of the British Airports Authority until 1972 when it was reinstated close to its original position. The photograph shows the cannon awaiting replacement.

Cannon at Heathrow 1998. The photograph shows the cannon back in place with the 1926 plaque now mounted on a sloping concrete plinth on the south side of the cannon. The plaque (see below) records the remarkable accuracy of Roy's measurement of the baseline - 27404.01 feet by his estimation 27406.19 feet as determined by the Ordnance Survey.

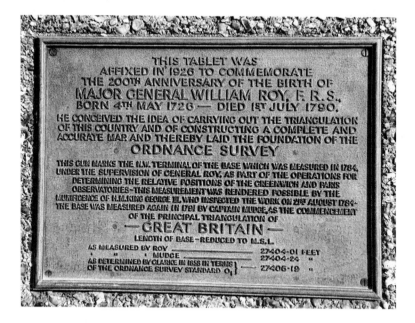

Roy was judged to have performed his task with *'a labour sufficient to derange a more than common degree of perseverance.'* He was therefore presented with the Copley Medal of the Royal Society in 1785 for the 'accurate and satisfactory manner in which he measured a base for operations of Trigonometry, upon Hounslow Heath.' Roy's account of his survey was published in the Proceedings of the Royal Society and the map shown on page 20 is a copy of that which accompanies his account.

Chapter Four

Agriculture in the Heathrow Area

For many centuries and long before aviation had ever been considered as a viable possibility agriculture was by far the principle activity in the Heathrow area. Harmondsworth Parish which included the hamlet of Heathrow was enclosed in 1819 and, before this, the area bounded by Heathrow Road, Tithe Barn Lane and the Bath Road was one of the open fields of the parish, known as Heathrow Field (see map on page 21). The area to the south and east of Heathrow Road was the common land of the parish and formed the western edge of Hounslow Heath. Although the Common was enclosed in 1819 the name persisted and the area was still referred to as such by older people in the parish until the final obliteration in 1944.

Heathrow itself as its name suggests was on the edge of the Heath bordered, on the western side, by the open arable fields of Harmondsworth Parish (see maps on pages 13 and 21). It was not in the centre of a blasted uninhabited heath as the aviation lobby is apt to suggest when seeking justification for its destruction to make way for the airport.

After the Inclosure the opportunity existed to up-grade the quality of the land and despite the proximity to Hounslow Heath with its notorious connotations of sterility the whole area developed into high quality agricultural land and was the centre of a prosperous market gardening industry. The brickearth soils which cover most of the area are light brown silty clays liable to dry into clods but friable when moist and with liming and manuring are capable of giving excellent results. The Land Utilisation Survey Report of 1937 (1) described them as being *'Some of the best in England and they are, and have been, extensively used for market gardening, although they are well-suited to almost any type of farming. In the national interest it is, therefore, a matter for regret that so much development of an urban and suburban character has been permitted to take place on this highly productive land.'*

The report went on to lament the fact that, 'at least four aerodromes have been recently established in the region three of them involving the conversion of excellent market-gardening land into grassland of little agricultural value.' The three aerodromes referred to must have been Heston, Fairey's at Heathrow and Hawker's at Langley. These are among the areas shown in stipple in the map below (reproduced from the LUS report) which denotes the areas lost to agriculture between 1914 and 1936, on this map the Fairey airfield has been circled by a dotted line.

Although regrettable, the loss of land to the airfield had little effect on the rural nature of the area and it can be seen, from the maps and illustrations in Chapter 1, that the Heathrow area represented the last significant tract of Grade 1 agricultural land in West Middlesex still in use for intensive production at the outbreak of war in 1939.

As will be seen later the lament of the LUS, and others like it, fell on deaf ears. Land which is capable of such intensive cultivation is of limited distribution and occupies less than five per-cent of the total land area of England and Wales. It obviously falls into the Grade 1 classification of agricultural land and in, a well-ordered society, would be regarded as a precious natural asset.

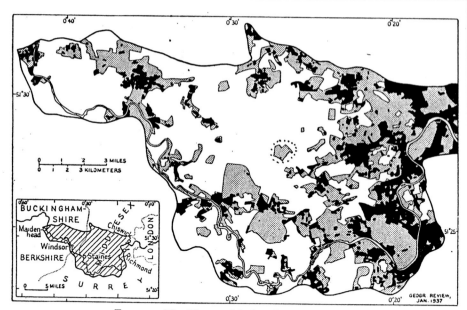

FIG. 32.—The Thames Market-Gardening Plain.

The solid line delimits the area of first-class arable soil which constitutes the region ;
the areas devoted to housing and industry in 1914 are shown in black ; the other areas which
have passed to non-agricultural uses by 1936 are shown in stipple ; only the blank areas
are now available for agriculture. Reproduced by courtesy of *Geographical Review*, published by the American Geographical Society of New York.

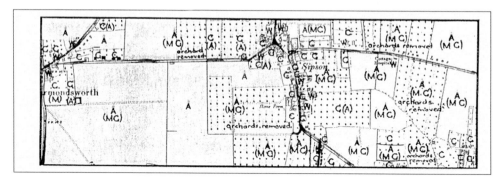

The Thames Valley Market Gardening Plain 1932. In the upper map the solid line delineates the
area of first class arable soil which constituted the region. The areas in non-agricultural use in 1914 are
shown in black. The stippled areas are those that passed out of agricultural use between 1914 and 1936.
The Fairey airfield (see page 62) in the centre of the map has been circled by a dotted line. Very little of
this area of Grade 1 agricultural land is now used for agriculture. 'The lower map shows a section of the
region in which modern building has only just begun to disturb the purely rural landscape whose almost
level surface is entirely devoted to market gardening and is divided into very large fields by the removal
of hedges. Cultivation is practised under the trees of the few remaining orchards, the majority of which
have been removed in favour of uninterrupted cultivation. The farmsteads are large and the big storage
barns attached to each swell the size of the neat little hamlets; the large building on the north of Sipson
Lane is a glasshouse used in conjunction with one of the market-gardens' (Excerpt from the Report
of the Land Utilisation Survey of Middlesex and the London Region 1937). Key: A (MG) = Market
Gardening; G = Orchard; G (A) = Orchards under which a ground crop is cultivated; G (M) = Grass
Orchards.

This is, of course, far from being the case; even the name brickearth for this highly fertile soil is derived from the fact that it can be used for making stock bricks. As Dudley Stamp pointed out (2), it is ironic that the name for this most desirable of agricultural soils should be derived from its use for urban development.

Fruit growing

By the latter half of the 19th century West Middlesex had become an important fruit growing area. The orchards planted in this period were mixed so that within one orchard there would have been apples, pears, plums etc. of many different varieties. In addition to tree fruit a large variety of soft fruit – raspberries, strawberries, gooseberries etc were grown; in many cases the soft fruit being grown under the trees in the orchards. The presence of the orchards greatly enhanced the flat landscape and was the subject of much favourable comment for example, Stephen Springall in his 'Country Rambles around Uxbridge' (1907) commented: *'Fruit trees we shall find to obtain in this neighbourhood for all round Harmondsworth, Harlington, Sipson and Heathrow are thousands and thousands of plum, cherry, pear, apple and damson trees in addition to innumerable bushes of currant and gooseberry which grow and flourish to perfection in the flat and open country.'*

After World War I fruit growing declined in importance, partly because of competition from foreign imports and partly because of the haphazard nature in which the orchards had been planned. In addition the expansion of market gardening in the district was making big demands on orchard land which, by 1939, had shrunk to less than 10 percent of its former area.

Market Gardening

Improvements in communications and the growth of London led, in West Middlesex, to a gradual change to market gardening from other forms of farming. It became easier to transport

LOT EIGHT (Coloured Green on Plan).

COMPRISES AN EXCEEDINGLY VALUABLE

Freehold Property

A CONSIDERABLE PORTION OF WHICH IS PLANTED WITH FRUIT TREES,

AND IS CONSIDERED ABSOLUTELY

The Finest Fruit Plantation in the District,

KNOWN AS

"Lord's Field,"

SITUATE AT

HEATHROW, in the Parish of HARMONDSWORTH, Middlesex,

CONTAINING ABOUT

57a. 0r. 36p.,

Abutting on the Main Road from WEST DRAYTON to BEDFONT.

Bounded on the North by the Property of A. Chordiar, Esq., Mr. T. Wild and Noel Headford; on the East by the Parish of Harlington; on the South by the Property of Mr. G. Parafield and the Harmondsworth Poor's Land; and on the West by the next West Drayton and Bedfont Road, to which it has

An Extensive Frontage of about 750 feet.

About 26a. 1r. 17p. are planted with Top and Under Fruit Trees of the very best known marketable kinds, in full bearing and in excellent condition, the remainder being

OPEN ▪ MARKET ▪ GARDEN ▪ GROUND

OF MOST PRODUCTIVE QUALITY.

Let on Lease to Mr. Charles Glover for 14 years from the 29th September, 1888, at the reduced Rental of

PER *£206 : 10 : 0* ANN.

The Property, which is in first-class heart and condition, is Tithe Free and Land Tax Redeemed, and is sold subject to the said Lease modified as to Rental as mentioned in the 4th Condition of Sale.

Sale of orchard and market gardening land at Heathrow, 1898. Note reference to finest fruit plantation in the district.

the products of this type of farming from more distant parts, while the growth of London's population increased the demand for market gardening produce, especially that of a more perishable nature. Thus by the time that it was overwhelmed by the airport West Middlesex had become an important gardening area with Heathrow itself virtually in the centre of what remained of the Thames Valley Market Gardening Plain (see References 1, 2, and the map reproduced above). As already discussed, the reason for this was that the brickearth soils of the Heathrow area by virtue of their texture, topography and drainage were ideally suited to intensive agriculture. But apart from this, the inherent fertility of the soils had been greatly improved over the years by the addition of huge quantities of horse manure arising from the immense horse population of London.

Up to the end of the 19th century all the traffic in London was horse-drawn and even in the 1930's horse-drawn transport was a still significant feature. The disposal of the horse-droppings would have been a serious problem had it not been for the fact that the market gardening wagons trundling into London each day with fresh fruit and vegetables were able to make the return journey loaded with manure. The amount of stable manure used by the market gardeners was immense and the Land Utilisation Survey reported that, even in the early 1930's when the amount of stable manure available was rapidly declining, an annual application of 20 to 40 tons per acre was not considered excessive.

As the horse population declined alternatives had to be found and one popular alternative was actually situated at Heathrow in the form of sewage sludge from the Perry Oaks sludge works (described later). An annual application of as much as 50 tons of dried sewage sludge per acre was used on some market gardens. A surprise feature of this was that tomato plants became quite common field weeds, as tomato seeds are able to survive human digestion and disposal through the sewage works.

Female field workers on Sipson Farm early 1900s. The journey of the vegetables from the fields to the market was a fairly complex operation. Workers in the fields would gather the vegetables (women, known as 'field women' usually did this job) and put them in boxes (baskets - made locally - were used in the earlier part of this century) which would be conveyed by a shuttle-service of horse-drawn carts (many of which were also made locally) to the farmyard. There the vegetables would be prepared ready for market, packed into boxes and loaded onto the market vans.

The LUS report pointed out that the market gardeners could justifiably claim that they actually made their soils, by a process which took many years, and few of them had anything to learn from soil scientists. They applied lime, chalk, farmyard manure, sewage sludge and phosphates and used appropriate ploughing techniques to bring their soils into the right condition to give the best yields of a succession of crops. The improvement in soil conditions was to such a degree that, valued in terms of capital improvements, the soil was often of greater value than the land on which it rested.

The market garden crops grown in the area included cabbages of various kinds, cauliflowers, lettuces, spinach, beetroot, turnips, parsnips, carrots, radishes, onions, leeks, artichokes, potatoes, marrows, peas, all types of beans and produce such as rhubarb, sea-kale and tomatoes which were grown in cold frames, glasshouses and forcing sheds.

Larger growers took produce to Covent Garden but several smaller ones were content with Brentford market which was nearer but not as profitable. Horse-drawn carts were used for the journey until the early part of this century when steam-traction engines were used by the larger growers soon to be replaced by motor lorries. When horses were employed the 14-mile journey to Covent Garden took about six hours and a carter would have to leave at 10.00 p.m. in order to arrive for the early morning market. At the market the larger growers had their own stalls from which they sold the produce and employed a man full-time to represent them in the market.

Ploughing Match, Tithe Barn Lane, Heathrow 1935. The rural nature of the area meant that Heathrow was the natural choice for staging the annual ploughing matches organised by the Middlesex Agricultural and Growers' Association. These were held in early autumn directly after the harvest. The last match ever to be held was the ninety-ninth which took place on 28 September 1937 on the farm of J.E. Philp and Son of Heathrow Hall on land in Tithe Barn Lane, Heathrow. In the following July it was decided to postpone the match arranged for October of that year because of a prolonged drought. Arrangements were therefore made in early 1939 for the hundredth ploughing match to be held at Tithe Barn Farm, Heathrow on 26 September 1939 but the outbreak of war three weeks earlier meant that this, too, had to be postponed. Matches were not resumed at the end of hostilities largely because most of the suitable sites had by then been buried under concrete.

Farm buildings at Sipson Farm, 1968. Messrs. Wild and Robbins of Sipson Farm was the largest
market gardening enterprise in the Heathrow area. The size and construction of their farm buildings
give a good indication of the prosperity of farming in West Middlesex. The farm was badly disrupted by
the construction of the M4 motorway and the airport spur in the early 1960s but carried on until 1970.
The farm buildings shown in the photograph were demolished to make way for housing development
about ten years later.

The farm of D. and J. Wild at Heathrow, 1944 (W. Wild). This photograph was taken just before the
wholesale evictions from Heathrow to make way for the construction of the airport. John Wild who
lived in the large house to the left of the glasshouses is leading the farm horse 'Captain' on the left of
the photograph.

Smallholdings at Heathrow, 1995. After WWI Middlesex County Council established 24 small-holdings to the west of the Perry Oaks sludge works. They consisted of small two-storey houses with steeply pitched roofs and eaves at first-floor level each with a plot of land attached. They comprised the Burrows Hill Close estate and Bedfont Court estate to the north of Spout Lane and were separated from each other when Stanwell Moor Road was built in 1948. Although in the shadow of the airport they survived until 2001 when the Burrows Hill estate became part of the T5 complex and the Bedfont Court estate was excavated for gravel. The top photograph shows one of the houses at the entrance to Burrows Hill Close, the lower (by R. McManus) shows farmland in Bedfont Court still in agricultural use with one of the small houses in the background. They effectively give the lie to BAA's claim that the terminal was only built on the site of a sludge works.

Remaining areas (marked in black) of market gardening land in SW Middlesex 1947, (based on a map in reference 4).

The effect of the airport on farming

According to the Greater London Development Plan of 1944 (GLDP), *'Although the airport (Heathrow) is on land of first-rate agricultural quality, it is felt after careful consideration and thorough weighing-up of all the factors, that the sacrifice for the proposed purpose of the airport is justified.'* The GLDP was written after the decision to construct the airport had been made and was a government-sponsored publication. As Mandy Rice-Davies might have remarked, 'they would say that, wouldn't they'.

In fact no consideration was given to the unique agricultural importance of the Heathrow area. This was the more reprehensible because Heathrow was at the very centre of the Thames Valley Market Gardening Plain. At a time of severe food shortages and stringent rationing this important market gardening area close to London should have been regarded as a valuable national resource and not one to be destroyed for the construction of an airport that could have been sited on land of lower agricultural potential.

The folly of destroying the valuable market garden land for the construction of an airport was well described by Dudley Stamp, the leading authority on land use and classification at the time. In a separate report (3) included in the GLDP he wrote:

'The brickearth is a magnificent soil – easily worked, adequately watered, of high natural fertility and capable of taking and holding manure. It is a soil fit to be ranked with the world's very best . . . In addition to the destruction of this good land by gravel digging a further using up has recently been made manifest where huge areas are taken for the construction of the airport. Was there ever such a profligate waste?'

The map shown opposite illustrates the huge hole initially left in the market-gardening land around Heathrow resulting from the construction of the airport.

The construction of the airport in 1944 involved the misappropriation of 1300 acres of agricultural land – 15 percent of the agricultural land in south-west Middlesex. Twenty growers were displaced either wholly or partly from their holdings. Subsequent airport-related developments have since made further inroads into the agricultural land in the area and the once-prosperous West Middlesex market gardening industry which has been virtually destroyed in less than a generation (5).

The fact remains that Heathrow is still a rich source of supply of fruit and vegetables and many of these are now imported into Britain from all over the world. It is difficult to justify both economically and environmentally the importation of foodstuffs which can be grown in this country.

Apart from the produce they supplied the destruction of the market gardens has changed the landscape from one which could be described in the following terms by Gordon Maxwell (6) in 1935: *'If you turn down from the Bath Road by the 'Three Magpies' you will come upon a road that is as rural as anywhere in England. It is not, perhaps, scenically wonderful but for detachment from London or any urban interests it would be hard to find its equal; there is a calmness and serenity about it that is soothing in a mad rushing world.'*

To one which could be described some 40 years later as: *'If there was an international prize for the ugliest landscape, some of the leading contenders would be around a number of the world's leading airports. this is partly because airports have to be situated on flat land which does nothing to hide the acres of concrete and partly because, for safety reasons, tall trees which might soften the skyline are not tolerated. As the more affluent owners flee from the aircraft nuisance – a nuisance which affects eyes, ears and nose – neighbourhoods decline and take on an unloved appearance. What we finish up with, all too frequently, is an unappealing wasteland of warehouses, car parks and poor housing. Anyone who has had the misfortune to spend time around the airports of London, Paris and Chicago will recognise the picture all too well'* (7).

References

1. Willatts, E.C., *Middlesex and the London Region*. Report of the Land Utilisation Survey No. 79. 1937
2. Stamp, Dudley, *The Land of Britain its use and misuse*. Longman, Green and Co. London 1948
3. Stamp, Dudley, *Land Classification and Agriculture*. Greater London Development Plan. HMSO London 1944
4. Bennet, L.G., *The Horticultural Industry of Middlesex*. Reading University, Miscellaneous Studies No. 7. 1952
5. Sherwood, P.T., *Agriculture in Harmondsworth Parish: Its growth and decline 1800-1970*. West Drayton Local History Society 1973
6. Maxwell, G., *Highwayman's Heath*. Thomasons, Hounslow 1935
7. Hudson, K. and Pettifer, J., *Diamonds in the sky*. Bodley Head and BBC. 1979

Chapter Five

The Perry Oaks Sludge Works

Origins

The origin of the works goes back to the West Middlesex Main Drainage Scheme inaugurated by the Middlesex County Council in the early 1930's as a result of what the Council referred to as 'the phenomenal growth' of the population of West Middlesex in the years following the Great War. Up to the development of the Main Drainage Scheme there was a large number of small and inefficient sewage works run by the individual District Councils and Boroughs. These were replaced by a large central sewage works at Mogden, Isleworth and a sludge disposal works at Perry Oaks, Heathrow. The main works at Mogden is in the middle of what even then was a highly populated area that would not have tolerated a sludge works as a neighbour. The sludge was therefore pumped from Mogden to a remote area of Heathrow some seven miles away where the settling lagoons would present less of a problem. With unconscious irony the surveyor's report claimed the site was chosen because 'it was isolated from existing dwelling-houses and the unlikelihood of building development in the immediate vicinity. This recommended the Perry Oaks site for sludge disposal although the low cost of the land (about one sixth the price of the Mogden land) was an important factor. Although only 7 miles from Mogden, it is no less than 3 miles from the nearest railway station. The nearest habitable dwelling is an isolated farm 700 yards from the drying beds; the nearest building development lies on the Bath Road more than half-mile to the north of the site.'

The original site at Perry Oaks was 220 acres in extent and was on the west side of Tithe Barn Lane, Heathrow. It was purchased by the County Council on 12 June 1931 for the sum of £33,000 from W. Whittington and Sons, who also occupied Perry Oaks Farm on the opposite side of Tithe Barn Lane. Before development the land was occupied by orchards as in the late 19th century much of West Middlesex had been given over to fruit growing.

The Sludge Works

Until the mid 1990s the works continued to occupy an enclave of some 250 acres on the western edge of the airport. At the main sewage works at Mogden, sludge was separated from the sewage and, after initial treatment was pumped over a seven mile distance to Perry Oaks. The sludge was pumped through a twin 12-inch cast iron main with an 18 inch cast iron pipe draining the works back to the Bath Road sewer. The pipes originally followed the route of the Bath Road and the former route of Tithe Barn Lane. Had the route chosen followed a more direct line by going across the fields to Perry Oaks it is quite probable that it would have rendered the construction of the airport too difficult to achieve.

MIDDLESEX COUNTY COUNCIL

INAUGURATION

OF THE

WEST MIDDLESEX
MAIN DRAINAGE SCHEME

BY

THE RIGHT HONOURABLE SIR KINGSLEY WOOD, M.P.

Minister of Health

After purchase the County Council developed the site as a sludge works and, together with the Mogden Works, it was formally opened by the Minister of Health, Sir Kingsley Wood at a ceremony held at Mogden Works on Friday, October 23 1936, although it had been in operation well before the opening date.

The Perry Oaks sludge works in 1946. The settling lagoons can be clearly seen in the lower half of the photograph which shows the original extent of the works. Construction of the airport to the east of works was well under way but as yet the northern and southern runways had not been extended on either side of it. Access to the works was originally from Tithe Barn Lane on the eastern side of the site but when this road was closed in 1948 access was made from the newly constructed Stanwell Moor Road on the western side. At the time of the loss of access from Tithe Barn Lane 53 acres of land were also lost from the south-east corner of the site. A report from the County Engineer dated 14 January 1948 stated that 'as a result of loss of capacity of the sludge lagoons now being removed from the SE corner of the Perry Oaks site for the airport extension, it will be necessary to provide replacement lagoons partly on site to the north-east corner of the works and partly immediately to the west of the Dukes River.' The extension to the west of the river took the boundary of the sludge works up to the Stanwell Moor Road. No further changes from the original boundaries of the site were made until the site was taken over for the construction of the Fifth Terminal.

The Perry Oaks sludge works shortly before closure in 1994. (J. Shane) The photograph shows the sludge works at ground level with the Duke of Northumberland's River which came up for air at Perry Oaks.

When it arrived at Perry Oaks, the sludge had a solids content of about 2 percent, and, in the original process, it was pumped into lagoons where the solid matter slowly separated under gravity and most of the water drained-off. After settling in the lagoons the volume and weight of the sludge was much reduced and it then had a solids content which had been raised from its initial value of about 2 percent to a solids content of 10 percent. It had also been changed into a product which is easy to handle and no longer offensive. The dried sludge was then removed in road tankers and spread, as a fertiliser, on agricultural land.

The method was a very cheap and efficient method of treating waste but suffered from the fact that it occupied a large area of land. Because of this, and the pressures to develop the site for the extension of the airport, in the mid-1990s Thames Water transferred its mode of operation entirely to a mechanical process for de-watering the sludge. This method required only 10 per cent of the space taken up by the original method

Although, when it first arrived, there were problems with the smell of the sludge, which could at times be offensive, the smell soon ceased to be objectionable. Visually the lagoons did not obtrude on the landscape and from a distance looked like any other open land. There were no buildings and the site consisted mainly of grassland, interspersed with water and scrub. For this reason, the sludge works were included in the Metropolitan Green Belt which was supposed to act as a 'lung' within the perimeter of the airport.

Apart from serving a valuable Green Belt function, in their original condition the sludge lagoons also attracted many birds and the site was an important habitat for wildlife. As a result Perry Oaks was designated as a 'Site of Metropolitan Importance for Nature Conservation' (SMI) by the London Ecology Unit. SMI's are 'the highest priority for nature conservation; they are of a quality which exists in very few places in London'. The sludge works together with the complex of gravel pits and reservoirs at the western end of the airport had also been proposed by English Nature for designation as a 'Special Protection Area' (SPA) under the EC directive for the Conservation of Wild Birds.

Access to the works was originally from Tithe Barn Lane on the eastern side of the site but when this road was closed in 1948 access was made from the newly constructed Stanwell Moor

Road on the western side. At the time of the loss of access from Tithe Barn Lane 53 acres of land were also lost from the south-east corner of the site. A report from the County Engineer dated 14 January 1948 stated that 'as a result of loss of capacity of the sludge lagoons now being removed from the SE corner of the Perry Oaks site for the airport extension, it will be necessary to provide replacement lagoons partly on site to the north-east corner of the works and partly immediately to the west of the Duke's River.' The extension to the west of the river took the boundary of the sludge works up to the Stanwell Moor Road.

No further changes from the original boundaries of the site were made up to the time that the works were closed in the late 1990s. The presence of the sludge works had proven to be a thorn in the side of the aviation authorities, which they had been trying to remove for the past 50 years. At last they had succeeded but the problems that this had caused are discussed in detail in Parts 2 and 4.

At the time of the first fifth terminal inquiry in 1983 (see page 130) both the British Airports Authority and the Thames Water Authority were public utilities ultimately answerable to the Government. Soon after the result of the inquiry was made known, both were privatised to become Public Limited Companies known, respectively, as BAA plc and Thames Water plc. This action markedly changed the attitude of both bodies to the possibility of developing the site of the Perry Oaks sludge works for a fifth terminal at Heathrow. Whilst it was in public control, there was no real incentive for Thames Water to move from the Perry Oaks site. The land had been acquired very cheaply at pre-war agricultural prices and there would have been no advantage to the Thames Water Authority to 'sell' it for development as it would have gained no benefit from the sale. Nor would the Government have gained anything as the 'sale' would have been merely a paper transaction, with the value of the Perry Oaks site merely being transferred from one public utility (TWA) to another (BAA).

The privatisation of both authorities completely changed this position and gave every incentive to both BAA plc and Thames Water plc to find an alternative to Perry Oaks for its sludge disposal. As Heathrow is by far the most profitable of its airports BAA, freed from Government policies that might run contrary to the expansion of the airport, was very keen to develop it to its maximum potential for the benefit of its shareholders. At the same time Thames Water would be in a position to gain a huge windfall profit if it could sell the land to BAA. From then on expansion was in the interests of the increased profitably of BAA, despite being at odds with local residents and environmental campaigners.

However, construction of a fifth terminal could not even begin before the Perry Oaks sludge works had been closed down and this could not be done until a solution had been found for the disposal of the sludge from Mogden which clearly has to go somewhere. Thames Water therefore began an investigation to find an alternative method for de-watering the sludge from Mogden which would require less space than the method as originally used at Perry Oaks. The solution to the problem was to de-water the sludge by mechanical means to produce a final product with a dry solids content of about 25 percent. This could be stacked within storage areas on site, using a mechanical conveyor system, whence it would be taken away and used on farmland in the same way as the sludge already being produced by the works at Perry Oaks. The mechanical de-watering of the sludge was put into effect at Perry Oaks in the mid-1990s which released 90 percent of the Perry Oaks site for other development and made it easier to transfer the operation to another site if, and when, the need arose.

The site chosen for the transfer of the sludge works was the Iver South sewage works. This lies to the south of the M4 between Junction 4b (with the M25) and Junction 5 (with the A4 at Langley) some two miles to the north-west of Perry Oaks. (The name of the works is misleading because it is a considerable distance from Iver and is much nearer to Colnbrook on the south side of the M4). The sewage works was already owned by Thames Water and occupied 15.5 acres. To allow for the expansion an additional nine acres was acquired bringing the total area to 24.4 acres which was less than one-tenth of the area occupied by the Perry Oaks works.

Chapter Six

Heathrow and Hatton – The Lost Hamlets

To make way for the airport in 1944 the hamlet of Heathrow and most of the hamlet of Hatton were demolished and their inhabitants were moved at very short notice.

Heathrow

Before 1944 Heathrow was the most remote and rural of the villages and hamlets that make up the large parish of Harmondsworth. Little modern development had occurred and a third of the 28 buildings in Harmondsworth parish listed by the Royal Commission on Historical Monuments were in Heathrow even though it was by far the smallest hamlet.

The settlement of Heathrow was spread out in a straggling manner on the west side of Heathrow Road from the Bath Road to Perry Oaks. Perry Oaks itself could almost be regarded as separate from Heathrow and it had direct access from the Bath Road via Tithe Barn Lane.

Although most of the agricultural la nd in West Middlesex was in use for market gardening, mixed farming was also practised at Heathrow itself. This made it more attractive than the rest of the locality as mixed farming, unlike market gardening, could in the 1930's exist quite happily with trees and hedgerows. The presence of numerous ponds and historic farmhouses added to its attractions.

It is impossible now to imagine the general tranquillity of the area as described by Maxwell and which John Keats, speaking of another part of Middlesex, likened to a *'Little noiseless noise among the leaves, Born of the very sigh that silence heaves.'* Nor is it possible to reveal the appearance of the hedgerows and verges which also added much to the rural scene. A description by Tony Harman of the hedgerows of Buckinghamshire in the 1920s and 1930s (*The Guardian*, 6th July 1989) could well have been written of Heathrow:

> *Early in the spring big white patches of blackthorn appeared, associated in people's minds with a cold snap, the so-called blackthorn winter; a false assumption though. Soon after came the may on the hawthorn trees. Not long after the last hawthorn petals had fallen, the hedges were festooned with honeysuckle and that lasted a long time, overlapping the season where there were wild roses everywhere, some pink some white.*
>
> *As soon as the roses had gone, bramble flowers were hanging off the branches. By September there were big dark purplish-blue sloes where the blackthorn had been, and blackberries where the bramble flowers were. And everywhere else red berries on the May trees (haws – but known as agars to the children of the Heathrow area); big bright red berries where the roses had been (hips); and round, red berries of innumerable plants one had hardly noticed before.*
>
> *Over it all were great drifts of what looked almost like human hair – Old Man's Beard. Its flowers had been green and inconspicuous, but you notice it in the winter all right, big strands and tresses of it.*

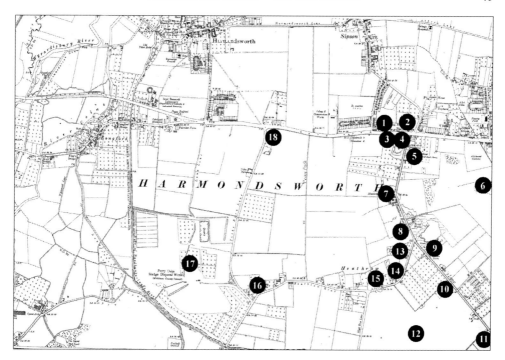

Heathrow – Principal Features in 1935. 1. Sipson and Heathrow School; 2. St.Saviour's Church; 3. Old Magpies; 4. Three Magpies; 5. Cannon; 6. 'Caeser's' Camp; 7. Heathrow Hall; 8. Palmer's Farm; 9. Wild's Farm; 10. Fairey Hangar; 11. Cain's Farm; 12. Great West Aerodrome; 13. Perrott's Farm; 14. Plough and Harrow; 15. Heathrow Farm; 16 Perry Oaks Farm; 17. Perry Oaks Sludge Works; 18. Shepherd's Pool.

'The Three Magpies' in 1926.

'The Old Magpies' 1935, demolished 1951.

Tony Harman does not mention the roadside verges but along the roads at Heathrow there was a drainage ditch under the hedge and then a wide verge, both of which were rich in wild flowers such as red and white campion, ragged robin, harebells, ox-eye daisies with willow herb and yellow iris beside the ponds.

Until 1944 a traveller following Maxwell's route and standing outside the 'Three Magpies' would have seen an even older inn, half-timbered and with a thatched roof that stood only 100 yards to the west. This was the 'Old Magpies' (No. 3 on map) almost opposite which was Sipson and Heathrow school (No. 1), opened on the Bath Road in 1877. Almost opposite the 'Three Magpies' was St. Saviour's Church (No. 2) opened in 1880 and now the site of the Heathrow Park Hotel. If he had then turned down Heathrow Road from the 'Three Magpies' (No. 4) he would have passed a row of houses (Doghurst Cottages) on the left, but after these the only buildings that would then be encountered were isolated farmhouses and cottages. The first farmhouse along the road was a rather undistinguished one on the left known as 'Bathurst'. As described in Chapter 3, in an orchard near to this house was a small fenced enclosure containing the barrel of the cannon marking the end of General Roy's baseline which was measured across Hounslow Heath in 1784 (5).

A little further along on the right-hand side of the road was one of the largest farmhouses; known as 'Heathrow Hall' (7) it was an attractive 18th-century building occupied by one of the several branches of the Philp family who farmed extensively in the area. The farmhouse adjoined a typical English farmyard with sheep, pigs and cattle and many old barns. Almost opposite 'Heathrow Hall' on the left side of the road was a large pond which had probably started life as a gravel pit to obtain road-making material. This pond was surrounded by trees and reeds and had a rich variety of wildlife including kingfishers looking for fish in the pond.

About a quarter of a mile past the pond just after passing Palmer's Farm, an early 17th century farmhouse on the right, the road forked at Wheatcut Corner. The road to the left, known as Cain's Lane, (Isaac Cane owned land on one side of the lane in 1819 – hence its name) led to East Bedfont and was dead straight, having been laid out across the Common by the Enclosure

Commissioners in 1819. On the east side of the lane were two modern farmhouses – Shrub End and Croft House – belonging to John Wild senior and his two sons David and John junior whose family had farmed in the parish for more than three hundred years.

The Fairey airfield, opened in 1929, was a little further along on the west side of the lane opposite yet another modern farmhouse occupied by F. W. Longhurst. Cain's Lane then continued until it was crossed in about half a mile by the Great South West Road, which had been constructed as a by-pass to the old Staines Road in 1930. The part of Cain's Lane beyond the Great South West Road was outside the boundaries of the airport and a small length of its south-east end still exists.

Coming back to the point at which Cain's Lane left Heathrow Road, which had been running roughly in a north-south direction, the road gradually swung round into an east-west alignment. About 200 yards along the road from its junction with Cain's Lane and on its north side was Heathrow's only public house, the 'Plough and Harrow', a small building of no great distinction dating from the mid-19th century. Soon after passing the 'Plough and Harrow' was a T-junction where High Tree Lane branched off to the left. This was another of the Enclosure Commissioners roads leading in a straight line to West Bedfont.

Half a mile along High Tree Lane at a fork marked on maps as 'Goathouse Tree Ford' the road crossed the Duke of Northumberland's river. The origins of which are discussed in Chapter 1. Goathouse Tree Ford was seldom, if ever, referred to as such and the area of the ford was known locally as High Tree River. It was a local beauty spot, popular for picnics, where children could safety paddle in the water and fish for 'tiddlers'. Although the very occasional traffic had to use the ford there was a footbridge high above the river, (the river had rather high banks, probably a result of the deposition of soil during its construction). The banks were well-wooded and on the south side was a riverside walk to Longford, about two miles away.

Coming back along High Tree Lane to rejoin Heathrow Road and almost opposite the junction were two cottages, laying back from the road, besides which was the entrance to 'Pease Path'. A public footpath ran across the fields in a northerly direction to join the Bath Road at a point between the Technicolor and Penguin Book factories, both of which had been built on the north side of the road in the late 1930s.

Heathrow Hall in 1935.

Demolition of Heathrow Hall 1944.

Shrub End, Cains Lane, Heathrow 1944 (W. Wild). On a corner of their farm and adjoining the road
was a corrugated iron mission hall which had been erected in 1901. This belonged to the Baptist Church
at Sipson and was the only 'church' in Heathrow, although there had been earlier churches at Heathrow
belonging to non-conformist sects. Standing are Mrs. D. (Naomi) Wild and the Rev. Griffith Lloyd
the Minister of Sipson Baptist Church. Seated are (L. to R) John G. Wild, his wife, son David and his
grandchildren James and Elizabeth. The family was evicted soon after and their houses demolished.

View from the window of Shrub End 1944 (W. Wild). The view is to the north-east and the shadowy rectangular shape marked with a cross is the large gas-holder at Southall about 4 miles away.

Cain's Lane area 1944 during construction of the airport. The view like that of the previous photograph is to the north-east with the gas-holder at Southall again marked with a cross. Cain's Lane runs across the top third of the photograph. The farm buildings seen in the previous photograph which had been on the far (east) side of the road have disappeared. The shed-like structure does not seem to be one of the original buildings and was probably erected by the contractors.

Surviving remnant of Cain's Lane, 2005.

The 'Plough and Harrow', Heathrow, *c.*1930. Demolished 1944 (D. Basham).

About another ¼-mile along the Heathrow Road, in an area of Heathrow known as Perry Oaks, the road forked again, the left fork, known as Oaks Road, led to Stanwell village. The right fork, known as Tithe Barn Lane, proceeded in a northerly direction to rejoin the Bath Road midway between the 'Three Magpies' and the 'Peggy Bedford'.

Just before the road forked and on its northern side, stood Perry Oaks Farm (No. 8), a most handsome red-brick Elizabethan farmhouse occupied by S. Whittington, a member of another old farming family in the locality. This farm had some very fine old barns, a dovecote and a duck-pond and was, without question, the best of the many farmsteads of Heathrow. Just past the farmhouse on the west side of Tithe Barn Lane was the Perry Oaks Sludge Works (No. 9) opened in 1936 by Middlesex County Council. This was nowhere near as bad as it sounds being some 200 acres of land occupied by lagoons in which the sludge was allowed to settle under gravity. Before the lagoons were destroyed in the late 1990s to make way for a fifth terminal at Heathrow the sludge works had become a site of some scientific importance because of the large number of wading birds attracted to the lagoons.

Tithe Barn Lane got its name from a barn half-way along its western side that was reputedly a reconstruction of a northern wing of the Great Barn of Harmondsworth. It is doubtful if, in fact, the Great Barn ever had a northern wing, but the story of the wing being dismantled and being re-erected in Tithe Barn Lane is often quoted. The area at the junction of Tithe Barn Lane and the main road was known as 'Shepherd's Pool' (No. 10), the pool being a large pond completely surrounded by trees. It had probably started life as a gravel pit but had become completely naturalised over 150 years when its name was recorded on the Enclosure Map.

The development of the airport meant Heathrow, most of Hatton and those parts of Harlington and Harmondsworth that lay to the south of the Bath Road, had to be demolished. The feelings of the residents of Heathrow who were removed from their homes are

Perry Oaks Farm, Heathrow, 1935. Demolished 1948.

Shepherd's Pool, Heathrow, 1927.

well summed-up by the poem written by John Wild whose family had farmed in the area for over 300 years. It certainly sums up the sadness and sense of great loss.

Lament for Heathrow

We shall remember thee in days to come
Before the ruthless hand of man had spoiled
When sweet peace lingered on thy country brow,
The day when sound of plover lulled thee,
The night when screech owl loved thy lonely shade
We shall remember thee although the time
Of visitation great had come!
No longer is there peace within thy gates
That peace which was thy birthright. Now they come
They strip the wealth and riches from the soil
Although most fertile land in all the south,
But now the tyrant's hand has claimed thee,
Cruel progress could not pass unheeding by.
Soon will be nought to mark thy hedges trim–
No hedge, no tree, no wayside flowerets fair–
Naught that is lovely left. Oh woe the day!
Long years have passed since Rome raised camp on thee,
And yet they passed and left thee undisturbed
Hadst thou a voice couldst tell us of thy past,
But now men want to rob of all thy grace
Full comely thou dost seem as we must go
And so 'Goodbye' – a long last farewell.
For some short time the larks may still come home–
The weasel, mole and field mouse tunnel round;
Yet as the circling days go swiftly by
Soon will be gone all traces of the past
Save in our memories fond – we still
Remember Heathrow.

John Wild 1944

Hatton

The hamlet of Hatton comprised the northernmost part of the parish of East Bedfont. When the airport was constructed in 1944 all that part of the hamlet that lay to the north of the Great South-West Road was obliterated; the southern part remained but developments brought about by the close proximity of the airport means that little of the original hamlet now survives. All of the buildings that were demolished were scattered along Hatton Road which ran from the Bath Road in the north and the Great South-West Road in the south.

Hatton Road – Principal Features, 1935 (based on 6in to 1 mile OS Map). The map is a continuation to the east of the map on page 112. The boundary of the airport as originally planned meant that the whole area bounded by the Great South-West Road, the Bath Road and Cranford Lane shared the fate of Heathrow. A = Harlington Corner, B = The Cedars; C = Hatton Gore; D = The Dog and Partridge; E = The Cyclist's Rest/Magpie Inn; F = Present-day site of Hatton Cross Station.

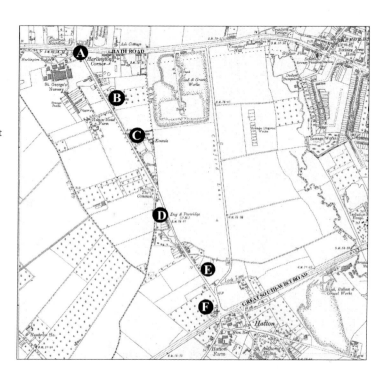

Hatton Road from Harlington Corner, 2007. About 200 yards of the original road alignment remains as does surprisingly the 1930s house on the extreme right (now named Stoic House and used as offices).

The Cedars, Hatton Road, c.1910 (HHLHS). This house was at one time the home of Mary Ann Cooper (nee Mitton) who was inspiration of Charles Dickens's character 'Little Dorritt'. As a friend of the family Dickens was a regular visitor to the house.

Hatton Gore, 1944 (HHLHS). In the 1930s the house was the home of Frank Kingdon Ward (1885-1958), a famous plant collector. He constructed a rock garden designing it to look like a bend in a river ravine in the Himalayas. It was built from York Stone acquired from the demolition of the old Bank of England building. During the 1939-45 the house was occupied by the Welsh Guards and briefly, before it was demolished in 1947, by the Home Guard.

'The Dog and Partridge', c.1930, Hatton Road (M. Russell). This was demolished in 1949 in the third phase of demolitions to make way for the airport. A new 'Dog and Partridge' was opened in Edinburgh Drive, Staines in the 1950s the licence having been held in suspense and transferred to the new public house by way of special removal. The lower photograph shows the licensee Henry Smith with his wife Eliza about to drive off to the brewery at Isleworth, their daughter Mary is looking out of the window.

'The Cyclist's Rest' (previously 'The Magpie Inn'), early 1930s (D. Rust).

Oliver Newall outside his smithy, Hatton, 1942. Until well into the 1940s horse-drawn traffic was still a common form of travel. Most villages of any size therefore had its own blacksmith and Hatton was no exception. Oliver Newall's forge was just to the south of the Great South-West Road and so survived the initial destruction but it has long-since gone. The boy in the trap is William Wild who had travelled with his father from Heathrow to the premises to have some repairs carried out by Oliver Newall. (W. Wild).

Farmland at Hatton, early 1944 (S. Heyward). The view is to the east with the houses in the background scattered along Hatton Road.

Desecrated farmland at Hatton, late 1944 (S. Heyward). Construction of the airport started in May 1944. This is from the same aspect but taken a few months after the previous photograph

The first half-mile of the road starting from Harlington Corner was in the parish of Harlington and included three large houses of note – The Limes, The Cedars and Hatton Gore all of which dated from about 1840.

Soon after crossing the parish boundary into Hatton proper on the west side of the road was a public house known as 'The Dog and Partridge'.

A little further on the opposite side of the road was a former beer-house known as 'The Magpie Inn'. This is an unusual name but even more so given that not very far away on the Bath Road were two similarly named inns 'The Three Magpies' (page 43) and 'The Old Magpies' (page 44). By 1914, possibly because of the nearby and larger 'Dog and Partridge' it had ceased to be a beer-house and had become a refreshment room and shop. In the early 1930s its name was changed to 'The Cyclist's Rest' by which name it remained until it was demolished in 1949.

Chapter Seven

The Growth of Aviation

Early Days

In December 1903 the Wright brothers were the first to fly a heavier than air machine and within a few years aviation achieved a phenomenal growth. The military significance of aviation was soon realised and the Royal Flying Corps (RFC) was founded in 1912 which by the end of the year had one squadron of airships and three of aircraft. With the outbreak of war the RFC was rapidly expanded; by 1916 it had 26 squadrons and a total of 421 aircraft. In April 1918 the RFC was amalgamated with the Royal Naval Service to become the Royal Air Force which by the end of the war had 22,000 aircraft.

Aerodromes for the RFC were established across the country with one of the first being at Stonehenge – perhaps the first indication of the lack of concern of the aviation lobby for the environment and the country's heritage! It was opened by the Royal Flying Corps on Salisbury Plain in 1917 and occupied about 1500 acres on either side of the Wylye – Amesbury Road (which is now the modern A303 – see map below). It acquired its name from the fact that it was immediately adjacent to Stonehenge and indeed it was even suggested at one time that the stones should be removed as they were a flying hazard. This may have been a tongue-in-the-cheek remark but in the light of subsequent events in the field of aviation probably not. In any case with the whole of Salisbury Plain to choose from it does seem perverse to have selected a site so close to Stonehenge.

The aerodrome closed in the early 1920s, the site then became derelict and was of serious concern to the National Trust which inaugurated a campaign to raise money to buy the site. The brochure, from which the map shown above is taken, describes Plot A as having for years been defaced by the derelict aerodrome and hutments. Enough money was obtained to buy all three plots of land and the site of Stonehenge secured against any further such depredations

With the end of the war in 1918 most of the aerodromes established by the RFC/RAF became surplus to requirements. However, the end of hostilities was accompanied by the growth in civil aviation so many of these former military airfields were taken over by private companies, one such was Hounslow Heath aerodrome.

Aviation in West Middlesex 1918–1944

Hounslow Heath aerodrome

Part of Hounslow Heath was used as an airfield by the Royal Flying Corps during the First World War when it was established on land belonging to the Army. The aerodrome was first used by the RFC as a base for anti-Zeppelin spotter aircraft and later as a pilot training airfield.

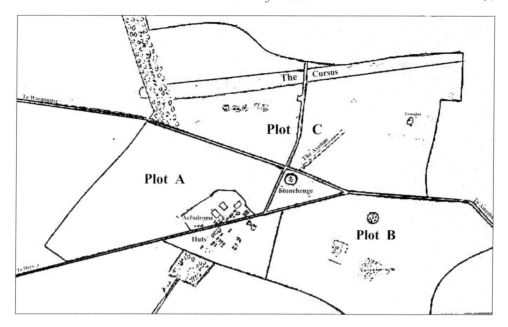

Map showing position of aerodrome in relation to Stonehenge.

Flying at Heathrow, Cain's Lane, c. 1903 (A. Glenie). This is probably the earliest record of any aerial activity at Heathrow. It shows a lighter-than air-balloon that had made a forced landing at Cain's Farm. Twenty five years later the Fairey Aviation Company opened its airfield in Cain's Lane close to where the balloon had landed.

Flying over Ashford in 1911 (G. Smeed). In 1911 the appearance of an aeroplane in the Heathrow area was such a phenomenon that it was photographed and published as a picture postcard. The flight probably took place over Shortwood Common.

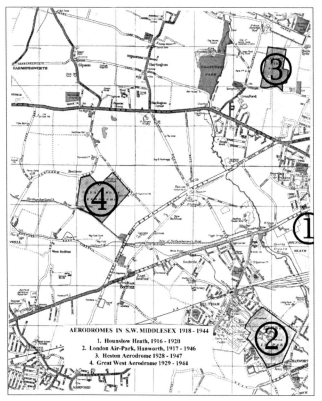

Aerodromes in Southwest Middlesex, 1916–1944.
The fact that the gravel and overlying soils that cover most of West Middlesex were deposited under water means that the land is flat and level in character with a general slope of no more than ten feet per mile. This makes it ideally suitable not only for agriculture but also for aviation. In addition it is close to London with relatively good communications and in the early 20th century it had a low population density. It was not therefore surprising that within a few years from the outbreak of WWI aviation interests should seek to establish airfields in the area at Hounslow, Hanworth, Heston and Heathrow respectively. Hounslow Heath airfield, which was the first to be established, had a very short life and had closed by 1920. One, the Great West Aerodrome, belonging to the Fairey Aviation Company, became the nucleus of Heathrow Airport and the other two had to close soon after because of their close proximity to the newly-established airport

On 1 April 1919 it was taken over as London's first airport and, soon after, the first regular flights from London to Paris began from the airfield. The first ever flight from England to Australia took off from the aerodrome on 12 November 1919 and arrived at Darwin on 10 December 1919 having completed the journey in 27 days, 20 hours, 20 minutes. Within a year the army demanded the return of the land allegedly for cavalry exercise. So the airfield closed in 1920 and all the services were transferred to Croydon which was to become the main civil airport for London until the Second World War.

Hounslow Heath aerodrome. The top photograph shows the aerodrome just before it closed in 1920. A plaque to commemorate the airfield was erected by the former Borough of Heston and Isleworth and unveiled by the Mayor of the newly created Borough of Hounslow in January 1966. It stands in the Staines Road opposite 'The Hussar' and is shown in the lower photograph which was taken in 1998. Since then it has been badly defaced by graffiti.

London Air Park, Hanworth

The association of Hanworth with aviation started in 1917 when Hanworth Park was used by Whitehead Aircraft Ltd of Feltham from which to fly their aircraft for test flights and deliveries. With the end of the war all flying activities came to an end and did not resume until 1928 when 229 acres of Hanworth Park were laid out as an airfield by National Flying Services Ltd with Hanworth House serving as the club house for the private airfield. About 1933 the General Aircraft Company came to Feltham and used the air park during the Second World War for their Hamilcar gliders and other planes. Flying ceased in 1946 because of Hanworth's proximity to Heathrow. In 1959 it became a public park owned by the local council.

Heston aerodrome

This airfield started life as a private airfield in 1928 when a private company – Airwork Ltd – bought 170 acres of land on the north side of Cranford Lane between the still rural villages of Heston and Cranford. The official opening took place on 6 July 1929. By 1934 Airwork Ltd was losing money on its operations from Heston aerodrome and, when it decided to sell, it seemed likely that the land would be developed for housing. At that time civil aviation interests were overseen by the Air Ministry which was soon put under pressure to buy the airfield and the surrounding open land so as to develop Heston as a viable alternative to Croydon – then the main civil airport in Britain – which was becoming too small to accommodate the expected increase in air transport.

The Air Ministry was very reluctant to become the owner and its first response was to try to persuade the County Councils of London and Middlesex and the Borough Council of Heston and Isleworth to take-over Heston as a municipal aerodrome to be run by the three local authorities. The Councils' responses were that if it was to be a national/international airport they could not see why they should be expected to bear the costs of development.

For example the Aerodromes Committee of the Middlesex County Council resolved, at its meeting on 19 June 1936, that it *'was unable to recommend the Council to proceed with the purchase of Heston airport either solely or in conjunction with the LCC.'* Interestingly at that meeting the Committee also considered and rejected an alternative proposal put forward by the Valuation Officers of the MCC and the LCC to locate a municipal aerodrome at Harmondsworth near the Perry Oaks Sludge Works which the officers *'considered to more satisfactory than Heston from all points of view. It was larger in area and would be less costly to develop; it could be extended by a further area of approx. 300 acres and the Southern Railway Stations at Feltham and Ashford were nearby affording good communications with London.'*

The action of the local councils in rejecting the Air Ministry's proposals put further pressure on the Ministry to acquire Heston. This was exemplified by an article in the 'Daily Telegraph' in August 1936 with an accompanying map (reproduced on page 64) which said:

> *Unless immediate action is taken, land on which Heston airport could be extended will pass into the hands of the builder. London would thus sacrifice an opportunity to possess an airport comparable with those of Berlin, Paris, Amsterdam and Frankfurt …Plans for the extension of Heston have been worked out in detail which is beyond the scope of a private company. If the extension scheme were saved Heston could have a runway of 1700 yards in a few months.*

The Air Ministry was unmoved and declared in September 1936 that *'there was no case for the purchase of Heston as a state-owned civil airport'*. However, pressure continued to be exerted and came to a head in October when the owners of the airfield lost patience and put it up for sale. In Novemeber the Air Ministry decided to purchase the airfield and much of the surrounding open land for the construction of an airport as a replacement for Croydon.

The Graf Zeppelin at Hanworth, 1932. Hanworth is best remembered, locally, by the visit of this famous airship in 1932. The top photograph shows the airship coming in to land and it can be seen on the ground in the bottom photograph which gives a good indication of its immense size. After returning to Germany, the airship which had been built in 1928, went on to cross the Atlantic on commercial flights until the outbreak of war in 1939. It was the most successful airship ever to be built and during its career, and unlike the ill-fated 'Hindenburg', it travelled more than 1 million miles without serious incident. It was destroyed during WWII.

Oddly enough, soon after the Air Ministry had acquired Heston, Middlesex County Council had a change of mind and urged the Air Ministry to develop Heathrow by expanding the Fairey aerodrome instead of developing Heston. The Air Ministry refused to consider such a proposal because of the difficulties in acquiring the land and went ahead with its plans for Heston. Expansion of the airfield at a cost of £2.5m was envisaged which involved the acquisition of land between the existing airfield and the Bath Road and what has since become the Parkway, increasing the area to 814 acres, the construction of a concrete runway 2000 yards in length and adding extra terminal capacity. Soon after Heston aerodrome became famous as the airfield to which Neville Chamberlain returned in 1938 after his meeting with Hitler in Munich.

The Great West Aerodrome

Charles Richard Fairey (1887–1956) began his aeronautical career by selling model aircraft to Gamages of High Holborn. In 1915 he formed his own company – the Fairey Aviation Company – which initially operated from factory premises in Clayton Road, Hayes. Fairey also bought a field in Harlington, bounded by Station Road, North Hyde Road and Dawley Road. The Harlington site was subsequently developed as the headquarters and factory of the company. A few flights were made from the field at Harlington but it was not really suitable and, from 1917, Northolt aerodrome became Fairey's test-flying base.

Heston Aerodrome in 1931. The view is towards the north-west; the road in the bottom left-hand corner is Cranford Lane which was the only access by road to the airfield. If the extensions proposed in 1938 had been realised the airfield would have extended beyond Cranford Lane as far south as the Bath Road (see map on page 64).

Farmland between Bath Road and Cranford Lane, c.1930 (A. Best). The view from the Bath Road looking north and shows the area of lane that would have been taken for the expansion of the airport.

Heston Aerodrome, 1935. This view is looking almost due south. The access from Cranford Lane can be clearly seen with open farmland between Cranford Lane and the Bath Road which is at the top of the photograph. This farmland also shown in the previous photograph was due to be swallowed up by the proposed extensions but, until very recently it survived in agricultural production. (Photograph courtesy of RAF Museum, Reference No. 5528-4.)

Arrival of Neville Chamberlain at Heston, 1938. Neville Chamberlain's flights to Munich in September 1938 were one of the first examples of 'shuttle diplomacy'. In all he made three flights from Heston for his meetings with Hitler. On the last occasion he returned with the notorious treaty signed by Hitler promising 'Peace in our time'. The photograph shows him reading the statement to the large crowd which had gathered to welcome him. (Photograph courtesy of RAF Museum, Reference No 5808-7.)

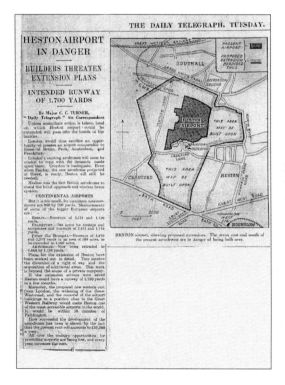

Heston Aerodrome showing the proposed extensions. Criticism of the Air Ministry's attitude to civil aviation reached a peak in 1936 when Heston airport was put up for sale by its owners and the open land around it seemed likely to be developed for housing. The airfield had started life as a private airfield in 1928 but by 1935 its owners had decided to sell it. The Air Ministry was soon put under pressure to buy the airfield and the surrounding open land so as to develop Heston as a viable alternative to Croydon. This was exemplified by the article in the *Daily Telegraph* in August 1936 which is reproduced here.

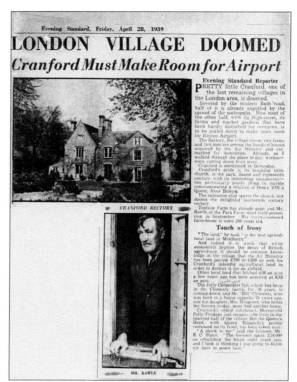

LONDON VILLAGE DOOMED

Cranford Must Make Room for Airport

Evening Standard Reporter

PRETTY little Cranford, one of the last remaining villages in the London area, is doomed.

Severed by the modern Bath 'road, half of it is already engulfed by the spread of the metropolis. Now most of the other half, with its High-street, its farms and market gardens that have been hardly disturbed for centuries, is to be pulled down to make more room for Heston Airport.

The Rectory, the village stores, two farms and two inns are among the hundred houses acquired by the Air Ministry and ear-marked for demolition. Already, as I walked through the place to-day, workmen were cutting down fruit trees.

Cranford is mentioned in Domesday. Cranford's pride is its beautiful little church, in the park, Saxon and eighteenth century, with its interesting monuments— one particularly lovely thing in marble commemorating a relative of Henry VIII.'s Queen, Anne Boleyn.

The extension plan spares the church but dooms the delightful fourteenth century rectory.

Tentlow Farm has already gone and Mr. Rawle, of the Park Farm, must yield possession in September. His crown-powered farm-house is some 200 years old.

Touch of Irony

"The land," he said, "is the best agricultural land in Middlesex."

And indeed it is ironic that while economists deplore the decay of British agriculture it should be common knowledge in the village that the Air Ministry has been paying £700 to £800 an acre for Cranford's splendid agricultural land in order to destroy it for an airfield. Other local land that fetched £36 an acre a few years ago has been acquired at £83 an acre.

The Jolly Carpenters Inn, which has been in the Clements family for 30 years, is coming down, and Mr. "Bill" Clements, who was born in a house opposite 75 years ago, and his daughter, Mrs Wingrove, who holds the licence to-day, must find another home. Cranford's oldest inhabitant, 80-year-old Polly Twinkle, just escapes—she lives in the bisected half of the village. But the Queen's Head, with Queen Elizabeth's profile embossed on its front, has been taken over.

"A shock to me" said the licensee, Mr. E. C. Stann. "The brewers spent £4,000 on rebuilding the house eight years ago, and I took it thinking I was going to finish my days in peace here."

CRANFORD RECTORY

MR. RAWLE

Threatened demolition of Cranford. This excerpt from the *Evening Standard* of 28 April 1939 refers to the demolitions that would take place as result of the proposal to extend Heston aerodrome. Work on the plan actually started in 1939 with the demolition of some buildings in Cranford and laying out the route of the Parkway. It had not progressed very far when war broke out in September and the plans for the construction of a new civil airport for London were seemingly abandoned for the duration of the war. But for this Heston would have become the largest civil airport in Britain by the end of 1941.

Northolt was owned and operated by the Air Ministry which in 1928 served notice on the company to vacate its leased premises which meant that it was forced to find another site for its experimental and production test flying.

The new site had to be within a reasonable distance from Hayes and, according to Peter Masefield the site eventually purchased was chosen because Norman Macmillan, Fairey's test pilot, remembered that a few years earlier in 1925 he had to make a forced landing in a field at Heathrow and later managed to take-off again without difficulty. He was impressed by the flatness and stability of the ground so, when he learned that Fairey's were to leave Northolt, he suggested that somewhere in the vicinity of this field would be an excellent choice for a new aerodrome. He made some aerial surveys of the area which confirmed his original impressions and Fairey's then made contact with the owner of the field and owners of adjacent fields. The maps on the next two pages show the extent of the purchases and the area of the airfield.

The Heathrow site was as close to the Hayes factory as was Northolt and proved to be just as convenient. It also had the advantage that the company held the freehold – little did Fairey know that the Air Ministry, having expelled him from Northolt, would eventually compulsorily acquire his new site at Heathrow! The airfield was known initially as the 'Harmondsworth Aerodrome' but later as the 'Great West Aerodrome'. It was renowned for its level and smooth turf and the hangar sited on the northern corner of the site was said at one time to be the largest in the world. However, this is hard to believe because it was not particularly large.

Due to the obvious advantages, the company decided to expand the site so that it could transfer the factory from Hayes to Heathrow thus bringing the works and flight testing facilities together. With this end in view Fairey's gradually acquired additional land, as opportunity occurred, and by 1943 they owned about 240 acres of land between Cain's Lane, High Tree Lane and the Duke of Northumberland's River. But for the war the probabilities are that there would, today, be an aircraft factory at Heathrow with an adjacent aerodrome and the proposed expansion of Heston aerodrome would have gone ahead.

Preparation of the airfield, *c.*1930 (B. Cockram). The fields purchased by the company were consolidated and initially sown with couch grass. Later the airfield was levelled and re-grassed by the specialist company C.P. Hunter and laid out as an area of high quality turf which was used for the first time in the late summer of 1930. The photograph shows some of the grass-sowing operations in progress.

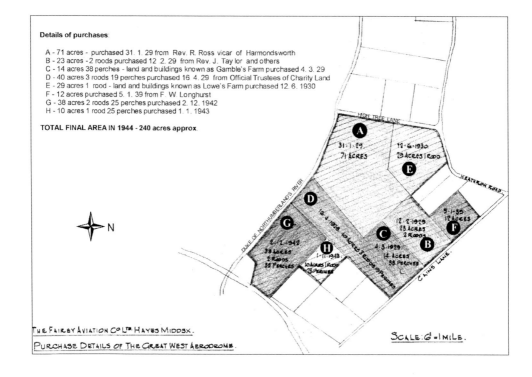

Details of purchases:

A - 71 acres - purchased 31. 1. 29 from Rev. R. Ross vicar of Harmondsworth
B - 23 acres -2 roods purchased 12 2. 29 from Rev. J. Taylor and others
C - 14 acres 38 perches - land and buildings known as Gamble's Farm purchased 4. 3. 29
D - 40 acres 3 roods 19 perches purchased 16 4. 29 from Official Trustees of Charity Land
E - 29 acres 1 rood - land and buildings known as Lowe's Farm purchased 12. 6. 1930
F - 12 acres purchased 5. 1. 39 from F. W. Longhurst
G - 38 acres 2 roods 25 perches purchased 2. 12. 1942
H - 10 acres 1 rood 25 perches purchased 1. 1. 1943

TOTAL FINAL AREA IN 1944 - 240 acres approx.

The Fairey Aerodrome, 1931.
The view is to the south-west with
the aerodrome occupying the top
quarter of the photograph. Apart
from the large hangar fronting Cain's
Lane there is little to distinguish
the airfield from the surrounding
agricultural land. What appears to
be road running diagonally from the
bottom right-hand corner is in fact
a farm track which joined Cain's
Lane just to the left of the hangar.
In the top right-hand corner is the
hamlet of Heathrow straggling along
Heathrow Road. The photograph
well illustrates the rural nature of the
area at that time.

Opposite below: **Acquisition of
land at Heathrow by the Fairey
Aviation Company, 1929–1943**.
The first land to be bought was
a 71 acre plot in the care of the
Vicar of Harmondsworth, being
held by him in lieu of the Vicarial
Tithes of the parish. The Church
Commissioners no doubt thought
that the money released by the sale could
be invested and produce an income for the
Vicar and his successors that would at least
be equal to any rent they could obtain from
the land. Would they have proceeded with
this, seemingly innocuous, transaction if
they had known that it would eventually
lead to a threat to the very existence of the
parish of Harmondsworth and the possible
destruction of its ancient church? Adjacent
plots were bought at much the same time
so that by the middle of 1929 the Company
had possession of nearly 180 acres of land in
Cain's Lane, Heathrow for which £28,000
had been paid. The last plot was acquired in
November 1943 only two months before
the company first learned that it was to lose
the land it had so patiently acquired.

Location of the Fairey Aerodrome.
The map shows the extent of the airfield
in about 1939 after an additional hangar
had been erected but before the company
had acquired the additional land to take
the boundaries up to the Great South West
Road (see previous map).

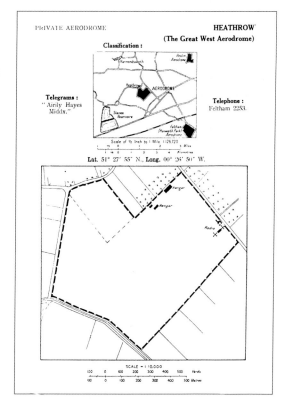

Royal Aeronautical Society's Garden Party, 1935. From 1935–1939 the aerodrome was the venue
for the Garden Party of the Royal Aeronautical Society. At these parties a wide variety of aircraft
were gathered from light planes to gliders, from military aircraft to new civil airliners fresh from the
production lines. There were also numerous aeronautical displays so that during the one day of the
party more people visited Heathrow than the total for the rest of the year. For example, *The Aeroplane*
of 8 May 1935 remarked: '*The Garden Party of the Royal Aeronautical Society at Heathrow Aerodrome,
Harmondsworth, on 5th May was a success in every way, in entertainment, in atmosphere, in attendance, in setting
– and in the weather. Most of the forthcoming season's exhibits have now been displayed in the best possible weather
and the most delightful surroundings. The aerodrome, which was kindly lent for the occasion by Mr. C. R. Fairey, the
Past President of the Society, is certainly one of the finest in the country. Its 'Hunterised' surface stretches away to its
distant hedges like a vast green lawn – and it made a perfect setting for frocks and aeroplanes alike. More than 2000
visitors – many of whom arrived by air in the serried rows of Moths which lined the Southern Boundary – had a
wonderful afternoon in the sun, rounded off by strawberries and cream in the shade of marquees.*'

The photographs on the adjacent pages clearly show that the presence of the airfield did little
to disturb the rural scene, it had no concrete runways, few buildings (at the outbreak of war two
additional hangars had been provided by the Ministry of Aircraft Production) and only a small
number of test flights. The airfield was, in fact, quite a local attraction as it was a novelty then to
see aeroplanes at such close quarters.

The Fairey aerodrome and the large numbers of people in the aviation world who visited it at
the time of the Garden Parties were undoubtedly what led the aviation interests to cast covetous
eyes on Heathrow as a site for a civil airport for London. However, if war had not broken out in
1939 it would have proved impossible for them to acquire Fairey's airfield and the surrounding
land. The war presented the opportunity for the whole area to be requisitioned and to begin the
development of a civil airport under the pretext that it was needed as a base for the RAF.

The aerodrome remained in use by Fairey for flight-testing until 1944. From the start the
company had hoped that the airfield would be, not only a flight-testing centre, but also a

FLYING PROGRAMME

May 14th, 1939

at

THE FAIREY AVIATION COMPANY'S AERODROME

(The Great West Aerodrome, near Hayes)

(By kind permission of Mr. C. R. Fairey, M.B.E., F.R.Ae.S.)

The following is an outline of the arrangements. They are subject to such alterations as may be found necessary at the time. Any change will be announced on the loud speakers.

|| It is particularly requested, in order that arrangements may run as smoothly as possible, that members and their guests will vacate their seats in the marquees as soon as they have had their teas. ||

p.m.

2.30—3.0 Reception by the President, Mr. A. H. R. Fedden, D.Sc., M.B.E., F.R.Ae.S.
(The reception is at the reception tent near the flagstaff and hangars)

Time	Firm	Pilot	Aircraft	Engine
14.50-14.58	Reid and Sigrist	G. Lowdell	Twin-engined Trainer	2 Gipsy Sixes
15.00-15.08	Vickers Aviation, Ltd.	J. Summers	Wellington	Pegasus XVIII's
15.10-15.18	Blackburn Aircraft, Ltd.	Flt.-Lt. Bailey	Skua	Perseus XII
15.20-15.28	Percival Aircraft, Ltd.	Cpt. Percival	Q.6	2 Gipsy Sixes
		D. M. Bray	Mew Gull	Gipsy VI
15.30-15.38	General Aircraft, Ltd.	D. Hollis-Williams	Cygnet, with tricycle under-carriage	
15.40-15.48	Boulton Paul Aircraft	C. Feather	Defiant	Merlin
15.50-15.58	Fairey Aviation Co.	F. H. Dixon	P4/34	Merlin Rm2M
16.00-16.08	Cierva Autogiro Co.	R. A. C. Brie	Type C40	Salmson 9Nd
16.10-16.38		TEA INTERVAL.		

During the tea interval there will be a demonstration at 16.10-16.24 by 9 Supermarine Spitfires of No. 74 Fighter Squadron, and at 16.26-16.38 a demonstration by 9 Bristol Blenheims of No. 601 Fighter Squadron of the Auxiliary Air Force.

Time	Firm	Pilot	Aircraft	Engine
16.40-16.48	The Willoughby Delta Co.	Capt. A. M. Kingwill	Willoughby St. Francis	2 Menasco Pirate C4
		S. Appleby	Schelde Musch	Praga B
16.50-17.18		TEA INTERVAL.		

During the tea interval there will be a demonstration of the following old types of machines:—

Time	Firm	Pilot	Aircraft	Engine
	International Horseless Carriage Corporation	R. G. J. Nash	1911 Bleriot XXVII	Gnome
	The Warden Aviation Company	R. O. Shuttleworth	Sopwith Pup Bleriot Deperdussin	Le Rhone Anzani
17.20-17.28	Westland Aircraft, Ltd.	Flt.-Lt. G. N. Snarey	Lysander II	Perseus XII
17.30-17.38	Tipsy Aircraft, Ltd.	Brian Allen A. D. Ward Capt. J. Youill	3 Tipsy's	Walter Mikron
17.40-17.48	Bristol Aeroplane Co.	A. J. Pegg	Bristol Blenheim	Mercury XV's
17.50-17.58	Fairey Aviation Co.	C. S. Staniland	Firefly II	
18.00		A.R.P. Demonstration.		

HONORARY MEDICAL OFFICER.

DR. NEVILLE WHITEHURST in attendance during the afternoon.

Flying Programme of the Royal Aeronautical Society, 1939. This is the front page of R.Ae.S. programme giving details of the displays which formed the most popular feature of the Garden Party. It was the last ever public function to take place at the Great West Aerodrome. Within four months war broke out and five years later the airfield was requisitioned by the Air Ministry under the pretext that it was urgently needed as a military airfield.

possible site for aircraft assembly, or even a complete new factory. Because of continued difficulties, including official opposition in extending the facilities, the airfield was never properly developed and, as described below, was eventually requisitioned by the Air Ministry in 1944.

The seizure of the aerodrome by the Air Ministry

At the outbreak of war Richard Fairey joined the Ministry of Aircraft Production and in August 1940 he was appointed as deputy to the Air Section of The British Purchasing Commission in Washington. In 1942 he rose to be the Director General of the British Air Mission in which capacity he remained until April 1945. This meant that in the crucial years of 1942–44 Fairey was out of the country at the time that the Air Ministry was conspiring to requisition his aerodrome at Heathrow. Had he remained in this country the outcome of the conspiracy to seize his aerodrome may well have been different.

Prototype Hendon bomber flying over the Great West Aerodrome, early 1930s. Fairey's hangar can be seen immediately under the bomber. The road running diagonally across the foreground of the photograph is Cain's Lane and in the background is Heathrow Road curling round towards Perry Oaks.

Even so it might be thought that, as members of the aviation community, the Fairey Aviation Company would have been given more sympathetic consideration than it in fact received. As the company were manufacturers of military aircraft during wartime, the Ministry of Aircraft Production would not agree to its eviction from the airfield without some alternative arrangement being made for the company's test flights.

Temporary arrangements were therefore reluctantly made for the company to use Heston aerodrome which was reasonably close to its factory at Hayes. However, this arrangement did not last for long and in 1947 for the third time in its history the company was evicted yet again by the Air Ministry. It ended up using White Waltham airfield in Berkshire more than 20 miles away from Hayes.

The effect of the prospective loss of their airfield on the Company can be judged from the correspondence that passed between Sir Richard Fairey, the founder of the Company, and his co-Chairman, Sir Clive Baillieu. Unfortunately for him, Fairey was out of the country at the critical time and when he first learned, officially, of the news on 7 January 1944 he cabled, '*Decision so utterly calamitous, suggest liquidation only practical prospect. However, detailed reply coming quickest route.*'

In his detailed reply Fairey wrote:

> *It is manifestly so much easier for the Civil Aviation authorities to look over the airports near London, that the foresight of private companies has made available, and then using government backing forcibly to acquire them, than to go to the infinite trouble that we had in making an aerial survey to find the site, buying the land from different owners, and then building up a fine airfield from what was market-gardening land. And why the haste to proceed? I cannot escape the thought that the hurry is not uninspired by the fact that a post-war government might not be armed with the power or even be willing to take action that is now being rushed through at the expense of the war effort ...*

Model aircraft flying at Heathrow, 1937. Because of his youthful interest in model aeroplanes Richard Fairey was very sympathetic to the requests of model aeroplane clubs to use his aerodrome at weekends when it was not being used for any other purposes. The aerodrome was the regular Sunday venue for members of the Hayes Model Aeroplane Club who flew their models at Heathrow. It was also used by other clubs which often travelled long distances to use the aerodrome One of the hazards for the model flying clubs was the Duke of Northumberland's river which formed the southern boundary of the airfield.

My mind concentrates on the fact that it is completely unnecessary for the Civil Aviation authorities to have their airport at Heathrow but it is vital to us. There are hundreds of airports in England, rapid transport by road and rail to say nothing of helicopter, could easily be made available to them, and within reasonable limits, the further they are from London the better can they operate. The exact reverse applies to us.

Part of the problem facing the Company was that the Defence of the Realm Act allowed the Government to requisition land without paying compensation. The question of paying compensation dragged on for many years after the war, as the Government took a very niggardly approach to the payment of proper compensation to the Company. Fairey's claim for compensation for the loss of the airfield raised many legal problems and made legal history. Since no legal precedent could be found, the compensation offer was on the basis of the loss of agricultural land. The company countered this by claiming that it was an industrial site and, as such, compensation should be made on this basis. Since the industrial site value was very much greater than that for agricultural use this claim was rejected by the Government. The legal battle continued until 1964 – 20 years after the airfield had been requisitioned! – when compensation was finally agreed at the sum of £1.6 million. By this time Richard Fairey had died (in 1956) but his son was later to say that *'the requisitioning of the aerodrome under wartime powers for civil use was a major scandal which my father never forgave. I very much doubt that he would have agreed to compensation of £1.6 million; the figure could hardly be said to have been generous even in 1964'* (John Fairey – private communication).

Sir Richard Fairey's gloomy prophecies, described above, proved to be well-founded and the Company was taken over by Westland Helicopters in 1960. Up to this time the company continued to use the White Waltham airfield but this was a serious handicap; the Heathrow airfield had been only three miles away from the Hayes factory whilst White Waltham was

The Fairey Hangar, 1961. The legal wranglings over compensation meant that Fairey's hangar at Heathrow could not be demolished until the question of compensation was settled. The hangar thus survived until 1964 and was the last of the original buildings at Heathrow to be demolished. The hangar is in the top right-hand corner of the photograph and is marked with a cross.

20 miles distant. The delays and increased maintenance costs in moving aircraft parts, for final assembly and flight testing, over the increased distance were a daily occurrence. These, over a period of years, must have seriously affected the company's profits and contributed to the take-over by Westland Helicopters.

After the take-over, aircraft continued to be built at the Hayes factory site until it was closed by Westlands in 1972. The site is now an industrial estate the greater part of which was, at first, occupied by Mercedes-Benz and Hitachi. Ironically these represent the two major powers that Fairey aircraft were employed to fight against in WWII – which raises the question of who actually won.

The name of Fairey in the locality has not completely disappeared from Hayes; it lingers on at the junction of North Hyde Road and Station Road which is still known locally as 'Fairey Corner' and 'Fairey Avenue' is a cul-de-sac off North Hyde Road.

PART TWO

The Growth of Heathrow Airport

Chapter One

The Wartime Origins

Although the Air Ministry was frequently subjected to severe criticism because of its alleged lack of interest in civil aviation matters, there was within the Ministry, unbeknown to its critics, a faction that was fanatically devoted to civil aviation. As events would show, they would go to extraordinary lengths to further its interests and the outbreak of war did nothing to deflect them from their plans, even if it meant diverting valuable resources away from the war effort. This faction was headed by Harold Balfour (of whom more later) the Parliamentary Under Secretary of State for Air between 1938 and 1944 who recommended, in a minute dated 23 May 1941, that an Inter-Departmental Committee should be set up to consider Post War Policy For Civil Aviation: *'It may not be too early even now to be thinking which would be suitable aerodromes which have special claims for civil aviation.'* This at a time when Britain stood alone and it was by no means certain what the outcome of the war would be and when everything was supposed to be subordinated to the war effort.

As previously mentioned, the idea of constructing a civil airport at Heathrow, rather than at Heston, had been first mooted in 1936, at the time of the acquisition of Heston. But the Air Ministry concluded then that it would be impossible to proceed because of objections from the Fairey Aviation Company (on account of its airfield), the Middlesex County Council (on account of its sludge works) and the Ministry of Agriculture. The outbreak of war presented the Air Ministry the opportunity to acquire the land compulsorily under the pretext that it was required as an airfield by the RAF and so avoid a public inquiry.

Although many thought at the time that the primary, if not the only purpose, of the development of the airport was for civil aviation the pretence that it was developed in response to the urgent need for a military airfield close to London is still officially maintained; even now most accounts give this as the reason for the development. It was not until 1973 in the autobiography (1) of Harold Balfour (later Lord Balfour of Inchrye) that the truth was finally admitted. Balfour made the astonishing claim in his autobiography that:

Almost the last thing I did in the Air Ministry of any importance was to hi-jack for Civil Aviation the land on which London Airport stands under the noses of resistant Ministerial colleagues. If hi-jack is too strong a term I plead guilty to the lesser crime of deceiving a cabinet Committee. Within the Department those of us who had studied post-war civil aviation needs knew that spreading out from the Fairey Aviation Company's small grass aerodrome on the Great West Staines Road was land ideal for London's main airport. We also knew that any thought of trying to get the land for civil aviation would have to go through complicated civil procedures and was bound to be resisted by Agriculture and Housing and maybe more Ministries. Therefore our only hope lay in taking over the Fairey field and adjacent land under wartime powers and regulations. These powers were drastic and positive and should not be employed for anything but war purposes.

By now with German defeat only a matter of time, Senior Staffs were planning Phase Two of the war which was to be our effort and contribution to the final conquest of Japan alongside our American Ally.

For this Phase Two, there would be much long range air transport of troops and supplies from the UK to the Far East. In six years aircraft had grown in size and landing speeds and now needed landing strips of ever increasing length. Arthur Street, my fellow conspirator, prepared a powerful paper for the cabinet saying that by requisitioning under war powers the Fairey field and a large area beyond we could ensure a service airfield from which all our Phase Two needs could operate. I confess now that in our hearts we knew of several bomber airfields in the Home Counties which could have been made to do the job just as well. The paper came to the Cabinet who referred the issue to a committee under the Lord President, Sir John Anderson. The Committee met and I represented the Air Ministry. I found that Beaverbrook who was still in the Government was also a member. I took him into my confidence as to the real reason we were pressing for what we were sure was London's best chance of a great civil airport. He played up well.

Rob. Hudson, Minister of Agriculture, put in a fierce objection on grounds that we were taking acres of the best market gardening ground. This I fear was very true. Ernest Brown, the Minister in charge of housing, joined Hudson in protest, saying we proposed to take land which had been earmarked for future housing schemes. I advanced as powerfully as I could the case for Phase Two needs. I did not dare to breathe the words 'Civil Aviation'. I put this right out of my mind so effectively that I really convinced myself of the priority of our case. The Cabinet came down on our side. We took the land. Hiroshima killed Phase Two. London Airport stands.

This account seems so improbable that, at the time it was given little credence, being seen merely as the idle boasts of a vain old man who had lost the wit to distinguish fact from fantasy and right from wrong. For example, another of his boasts was that as a fighter pilot in the 1914–18 war he had shot down a German observer balloon and deliberately killed the occupant when his unfortunate victim attempted to parachute to safety. His grounds for such inhuman behaviour were that the observer would have resumed his activities if he had been allowed to escape. [It is worth noting that even a major war criminal, such as Hermann Goering, was appalled by this practice and he instructed his Luftwaffe pilots that they were not to kill their opponents in this manner].

Balfour's account certainly does not correspond with the account given by Douglas Jay in his autobiography (2) in which he records, *'In my last months with the Ministry of Supply. I was asked to attend a meeting at the Air Ministry to decide on a site for a post-war civil airport, I protested at first that this was no business of mine at this stage of the war. But I was ordered to go and about six of us assembled at Assistant Secretary level. The meeting lasted forty minutes and we decided on Heathrow.'* In the next sentence he contrasts the speed of that decision with the later search for a third airport site. *'In the 1960's and 1970's the Government and Parliament discussed for fifteen years the location of a third London Airport, spent several millions on public inquiries and by the late 1970's we had no new decision and no new airport.'*

Jay also declared in his autobiography that *'The gentleman in Whitehall really does know best'* (he was later as President of the Board of Trade a leading proponent of Stansted), and fails to realise that the agonising over the site of a third airport was due to the horrific environmental consequences of the decision to choose Heathrow as the site of the first airport. In any case it is now apparent that Jay's account is incorrect and that he was referring to a meeting which took place on 7 March 1945 when the construction, ostensibly as a military airfield, was well under way.

This much is known from the Air Ministry files, now in the PRO, which make it abundantly clear that Balfour's account is substantially correct except in one important respect. The important, if perhaps not surprising (given his odd sense of values), omission in Balfour's account is that he was not the prime instigator. In fact the origin of Heathrow came from S.A.Dismore, who, pre-war, had been Assistant General Manager of Imperial Airways (which became the British Overseas Airways Corporation (BOAC) in 1939). On the outbreak of war he joined the RAF and in December 1942 he wrote an internal memorandum stating the alleged need for a new major airport for air transport operations in the London area and that Heston was probably the most suitable answer *'but Heathrow is also a possibility'*. With his background it is obvious that he had in mind an airport for civil use and in fact it was the Corporation that was the instigator of the original plans. In early 1943, it made a survey of the area and came up with proposals for a civil airport at Heathrow which it presented to the Air Ministry.

The Ministry was a very willing co-conspirator but, realising that it could not possibly acquire the land for the development of a civil airfield, it had to resort to the pre-text that the land was needed for a military airfield so that it could be compulsorily requisitioned under the terms of the Defence of the Realm Act. To begin with the Air Ministry was happy for BOAC to be represented at the Heathrow development meetings. Later, becoming alarmed that BOAC's grandiose plans might divulge the real reason for the development, the Air Ministry excluded the Corporation which led to friction between the two parties when BOAC learned of the final plans which did not accord with what it regarded as its own requirements.

This can be seen from an Air Ministry internal minute stating that:

> There has been a good deal of complaint with Heathrow from BOAC which has put forward alternative pro-
> posals for the development of the site …the Corporation has not ceased to complain that full weight is not being

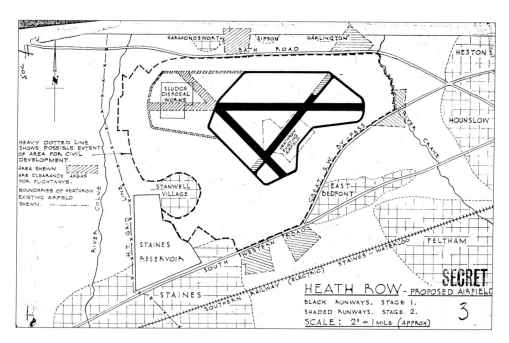

Initial proposals for the airport, 1943 (from National Archives File No. AVIA2/2269). The proposals involved the re-siting of the Perry Oaks sludge disposal works and show the runways to be constructed as part of the Stage 1 development in black. The main east-west runway on the map was to be further south of the Bath Road with the sludge works to be incorporated as part of the Stage 2 development. Evidence that the airport was envisaged from the outset as being for civil use can be seen from the map which shows the proposals for the airport drawn up in October 1943 and which were later submitted to the War Cabinet for approval. This gives the boundary of the possible extent of the area to be taken up for civil development.

given to its views. But as the present plan is a purely military project, this plan has not been discussed with the Corporation. Indeed since Fairey's are being displaced under war-time powers, much against their will, it is most important, until the civil scheme is approved by Government, to preserve the position that the present plan is a purely military one not open to criticism by BOAC.

Further evidence of the degree of bad feeling which eventually arose between them can be seen from a letter sent by the Ministry to the Corporation on 11 December 1943 reminding it that:

The governing members of BOAC are not the responsible authority for the provision of an up-to-date London airport for use by civil aviation after the war. The BOAC Act 1939 states that 'The Corporation shall not, except with the authority of an order by the Secretary of State for Air, acquire or control any aerodrome in the British Isles so far no such order has been made by the Secretary of State nor has the need for such a course arisen.'

The proposals for development envisaged construction in three stages, and at a meeting of the Anderson Committee (i.e. the one to which Balfour refers) a recommendation was passed on to the War Cabinet that approval to develop Stage 1 should be given. At a meeting two days later on 12 November 1943 the War Cabinet provisionally accepted this recommendation. This opened the way for the development to begin but, as will be seen later, there were still several difficulties to be overcome including worries about the legality of the action being taken. On this point advice was sought from the Treasury Solicitor in a minute dated 4 February 1944 which gives the information that:

On the matter generally you should be aware that the ultimate object is to provide a suitable (civil) airport for London. Were there no other object it would be a question of Civil Aviation only and presumably Defence Regulations could not have been used for obtaining provision of land for use for normal peace-time purposes.

The solicitor's reply is not preserved in the files but the minute leaves no doubt of the true intentions of those concerned within the Air Ministry who pursued their aim with a fanatical zeal even though it meant diverting valuable resources away from the war effort at a time when the preparations for the Normandy landings were well under way.

Inhibiting factors

Two factors inhibited the Air Ministry's proposals: one was the presence of the sludge disposal works at Perry Oaks, the other was the attitude of Winston Churchill. Other factors which might be thought would have played a part, such as the problem of aircraft noise, the fate of the inhabitants who were to be evicted from their homes, the effects on the Fairey Aviation Company and on agriculture, were completely ignored. The effects of the development of the airport on Fairey's and on the important West Middlesex market gardening industry have already been considered in Part 1. The remaining factors are considered in this Section.

Noise: In view of the major problems caused by aircraft noise it is quite extraordinary that there is no mention of noise anywhere in the files and the problem seems to have been entirely ignored. Colin Buchanan (3) has commented on this strange omission and one can do no better than to quote him on this:

There were so many unbelievably noisy aircraft around in 1944 that it seems incredible that a so potent side-effect of aviation could have been overlooked. But overlooked it was. Heathrow was developed with a pair of parallel runways running due east-west pointing in one direction at point-blank range straight into the huge housing mass of West London and in the other direction, straight at Windsor only six miles away – Windsor of all places, historic town, royal residence, famous schools, glorious stretch of river, parks and gardens beyond compare. Heathrow is fifteen miles from the middle of London. This comparatively close proximity to the heart of a big city has presumably paid dividends over the years in respect of reduced travelling time to and from the airport, but the misery which the flight paths have spread, also over many years, far and wide over a huge part of London and the Home Counties, must surely make that decision in 1943 the most disastrous planning disaster to hit our country.

In this disaster area live half a million people, whose daily lives are constantly disrupted by aircraft noise. The very layout of Heathrow is an affront to the rights and well-being of those who live under the airport's flight paths. 'Tolerate or emigrate' are not options for these people or places. (Here are Windsor Castle, Hampton Court, Chiswick House, Kew Gardens, Richmond Park, Syon Park and Osterley Park all historic and attractive places severely disturbed by overflying aircraft).

Aircraft noise consists of a build-up to a peak level, occurring at intervals, as opposed to the continuous but fluctuating noise from heavy traffic. The annoyance caused by aircraft depends on the peak perceived noise levels and on the number of aircraft heard within a given period.

The index used in this country, until 1990, to define the annoyance was the so-called 'Noise and Number Index' (NNI). This index has since been replaced by the 'Equivalent Continuous Sound Level' (L_{eq}) with 57 L_{eq}, which represents the equivalent continuous sound level measured in A-weighted decibels (dBA). The Leq method of assessment averages out exposure to noise over a number of hours. On that basis a figure of 57 dBA L_{eq}, which corresponds approximately to 35 NNI, is claimed to correlate to the onset of annoyance. Contours of noise exposure in terms of NNI or L_{eq} can be mapped out around an airport in a similar manner to the contour lines used on maps to signify differences in height (see below). An official committee set up to consider the problem of noise concluded, well before aircraft noise had become a widespread problem, that extensive annoyance is caused when the noise exposure exceeded 35 NNI and the noise became intolerable above the range 50-60 NNI. However, more recent research (4) has brought this figure into question and this showed that:

- For areas with L_{eq} less than around 43dBA, the proportion of respondents who were at least very annoyed was less than 12%.
- The proportion of respondents at least very annoyed generally increased with L_{eq} for values of L_{eq} over 43dBA, although there was a relatively large spread in percentages for most L_{eq} values.
- For areas with L_{eq} greater than 57dBA, more than 60% of respondents were at least very annoyed.

This more recent study showed that 50dBA would be a more realistic figure to use as 60% of respondents were *very* annoyed at a noise level of 57db. This should be compared with the 1990 study that gave a value of 57db as merely the *onset* of annoyance. Perhaps not surprisingly the Department for Transport was very reluctant to see this report published. This difference of 7dB might suggest a difference of only 14% in noise levels but this is grossly misleading as the decibel is not a linear scale. It is in fact a logarithmic scale and a perceived noise level of 57db is perceived by the human ear as being four times as loud as a level of 50db.

The fate of the inhabitants: The first official intimation of possible eviction of the local residents was the receipt of the letter from the Air Ministry in May 1943 which is reproduced above. This was followed-up by a letter, shown below, giving notice to quit which was clearly intended to be sent in February 1944 but was not, in fact posted until 2 May 1944. The delay in sending the second letter was undoubtedly due to the receipt on 12 February of Churchill's minute to the Air Ministry, referred to in the next section, which led to a delay in final approval until 13 April.

The welfare of the people to be evicted to make way for the airport received scant consideration from the authorities. Many of them came from families who had lived in the Heathrow area for generations.

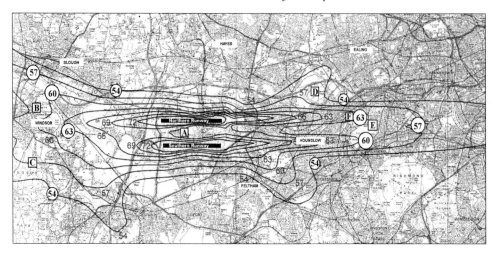

Leq noise contours around Heathrow in relation to areas of High Amenity value. The map shows the estimated noise contours for a two runway airport with 480,000 air traffic movements annually. 57 Leq corresponds to aircraft overflying at intervals of 15 minutes with intrusive levels of noise inside houses. (Noise contours based on information published by the Department for Transport). Key: A = Heathrow Airport; B = Windsor Castle; C = Windsor Great Park; D = Osterley Park and House; E = Kew Gardens; F = Syon Park and House; Circled figures = Noise Contours in Leq.

Noise Band (dBA)	2001	2003
55–59	306300	311500
60–64	91500	96900
65–69	28100	33500
70–74	3400	3900
Total > 55dBA	**429400**	**446200**

Number of people living within each noise band. (From: Civil Aviation Authority, *ERCD Report 0306: Noise Mapping – Aircraft Traffic Noise* (February 2004), Table 3.1.5). Even official estimates show that half a million people around Heathrow live within the 55 Leq contour which stretches from Maidenhead in the west to Fulham in the east. A more realistic estimate is about 2 million. For those living close to the airport the situation is of course much worse and the Inspector reporting on the 4th Terminal Inquiry (described later) concluded that, 'In my view the present levels of noise around Heathrow are unacceptable in a civilised society.'

1 May 2007

Low-flying aircraft over Windsor Castle, 2007. The castle is almost directly in line with the northern runway (see map on previous page). Windsor, the Castle and the Great Park, areas of immense interest to tourists, suffer severely from aircraft noise.

Low flying aircraft over Kew Gardens. Kew Gardens is the oldest and one of the finest botanical gardens in the world and is a World Heritage Site but like Windsor it suffers severely from aircraft noise. World Heritage Sites have 'outstanding universal value' and the 1972 World Heritage Convention aims to protect the values of these unique cultural or natural sites, however, it is has not protected Kew against the noise inflicted by the aviation industry.

TELEPHONE: **HOLBORN 3434**
Extn. ....

Any communications on the
subject of this letter should
be addressed to:—

THE SECRETARY,

and the following number
quoted:—

A.535303/43/W.6.b.(3).

AIR MINISTRY,

LONDON, W.C.2.

May, 1943.

Sir,

    I am directed to inform you that Air
Ministry have under consideration the construction
of an airfield in the Harmondsworth-Bedfont area, and
from a recent survey it appears that property in your
ownership or occupation is likely to be affected.
I have to state that this survey is only of a
preliminary nature and should it be decided to proceed
with the matter a further communication will be
addressed to you.

    I am, Sir,
    Your obedient Servant,

for Director of Lands & Requisitioning.

Letter of May 1943 giving preliminary notice to residents of the Air Ministry's intentions to requisition their properties.

Temple Bar 5411
XXXHolborn 3434.
Extn. 0134

TELEPHONE:

Any communications on the
subject of this letter should
be addressed to:—

THE UNDER SECRETARY
OF STATE, AIR MINISTRY,
and the following number
quoted:—

A.63213/44/W.6.b.3./R.88.

AIR MINISTRY,

LONDON, W.C.2.

2nd May
~~February,~~ 1944.

Your Ref. ....

Sir,   Property at Heath Row.

    I am directed to inform you that the airfield at Heath Row
is to be enlarged in the near future and it will be necessary
for this purpose to take over your property possession of which,
it is anticipated, will be required not later than 5h-7-1944
Formal Notice of Requisition, in duplicate, is enclosed, one
copy of which should be signed and returned in the accompanying
franked envelope.

    Three copies of Claim Form 1, in respect of your interest as
occupier, are also enclosed which, on completion, should be
returned, in duplicate, to the Air Ministry. In this connection,
it is pointed out that under Section 11 of the Compensation
(Defence) Act, 1939, your claim must be lodged within six months
from the date on which the compensation accrues due, that is,
the date on which possession is taken, as otherwise it will not be
entertained.

    Before any work is done on the property a Lands Officer
will visit the site and discuss with you detailed arrangements
for taking possession. Subject to essential Air Ministry
requirements, every facility will be given to enable you to remove
your movable property and effects and any growing crops.

    The property is being taken over under the Defence Regulations
but this will not preclude sale and purchase by agreement if the
Air Ministry decides that it is required for permanent retention.

    In conclusion, I am to draw attention to the fact that the
Defence Regulations prohibit the making of any sketch, plan or
other representation of any prohibited place. This prohibition
applies to the making of any sketch or plan of R.A.F. Stations
or defence works, etc., or the marking on any such sketch or plan
of any Stations or works.

    I am, Sir,
    Your obedient Servant,

for Director of Lands and Requisitioning.

D.J. Wild, Esq.,
Shrub End,
Cains Lane,
Heathrow Road,
West Drayton.
Middx.

Letter dated 2 May 1944, giving notice of eviction (W. Wild). The cold-hearted letter gave only two months for the owner of the farm to settle up his affairs and vacate his property. With typical civil service jargon and unconscious irony it is signed by somebody who describes himself as the recipient's obedient servant! David Wild's family had lived in the area for the previous 400 years.

The Air Ministry was indeed loath to accept any responsibility for them at all and tried to get the Ministry of Health (then responsible for housing) and the local authorities to find alternative accommodation at a time when these bodies were desperately engaged on re-housing people whose houses had been destroyed by the V1 attacks on London. Faced with the refusal of these organisations to help, the Ministry even considered the possibility of forcibly billeting the unfortunate people in other houses in the area with all the problems that would have entailed. In the end the Ministry used accommodation already in its possession or in the possession of other service Ministries and most refugees from the Stage 1 development were re-housed at Heston in property adjoining the aerodrome.

The feelings of the refugees as they left their homes for the last time are well summed-up by the lament written by one of them which is reproduced at the end of Part 1.

In the case of landowners their property was requisitioned, but not purchased, as the Defence Regulations envisaged that in many cases the requisitioned property would be returned to its original owners after the war. The owners were therefore paid a compensation rental by the Government on the supposition that they had let their land and property to the authorities for the duration of the war. In the case of Heathrow there was, of course, never any intention of returning the land to its rightful owners but the hypocritical pretence was made that it might be. Consequently the landowners did not receive proper compensation until well after the war and even then only at pre-war values.

Apart from this the terms of compensation were extremely harsh. One farmer, before he left, took away his greenhouses and sheds ; the value of these was deducted from his eventual compensation even to the extent that the value of his front gate and hedge, which he also removed, was taken into account. Had he left them in place they would have been destroyed as they were of no value to the Air Ministry. The same attitude was adopted in awarding compensation for growing crops which were regularly inspected by the Air Ministry before the owners were evicted. In one case a deduction was made, *'because the crop (of broad beans) was seriously affected by black fly…and my notes show that the crop of lettuce had not been watered.'* As if a farmer would regularly spray his beans and water his lettuce when he knew full well that they were likely to be destroyed before they reached maturity!

When it came to finding accommodation for people being evicted for later developments the Ministry and later the Ministry of Civil Aviation adopted the knock-on-the-door approach of personal interview to find the number of people involved and to ascertain their personal circumstances. The same callous attitude was adopted as can be seen from a minute on the files addressed to the interviewers to the effect that, 'Initial contact made with occupiers is most important as the compensation finally paid is often affected by the antagonism or goodwill set up at the first meeting.'

The general feeling of helplessness in the face of the cold-hearted attitude first of the Air Ministry and later of the Ministry of Civil Aviation is well summed up in an editorial reproduced below under the title of 'Wiped off the Map' in the Middlesex Advertiser and Gazette dated 5 December 1947. This editorial refers specifically to the proposed evictions for the Stage 3 development north of the Bath Road which was eventually abandoned (see later) but it could well have been written at any time between 1944 and 1951.

The Perry Oaks Problem: The proposals drawn up by the Air Ministry and approved at the first meeting of the Anderson Committee involved the resiting of the Perry Oaks sludge disposal works. The map on page 75, dated October 1943, shows the runways to be constructed as part of Stage 1 of the development in black. The main east-west runway on the map is further south of the Bath Road than at present with the sludge works being incorporated into the airport as part of the Stage 2 development.

The Defence of the Realm Act 1939 which was used to acquire the land for development allowed the authorities to requisition at short notice land deemed to be needed in connexion with the pursuit of the war without any right of appeal. In theory the sludge works could

WIPED OFF THE MAP

An atomic bomb dropped at Heathrow could not spread devastation more widely than the disruption caused by (the construction of an) airport on this spot. True the bomb would do it in no time at all but the fact that the extension of the airport is to be effected in a matter of years only ensures that the sterilization will be more thorough. Ancient townships, valuable farmland, a huge section of the Great South West Road, every sort of building old and new, is to be swept utterly away and not even a living tree is to remain in seven square miles of the expanse thus blighted.

Heathrow has gone, soon Sipson will be nothing but a memory and Harlington with its venerable buildings and fruitful orchards will be engulfed in turn. West Drayton, Harmondsworth, Stanwell and other communities are to suffer encroachment and their surviving portions will have the airport brought to their doorsteps with the shattering roar of transatlantic monsters.

Where does the individual stand in all this - the farmer on his land, the family in the home, the worshipper in the church, all the units of life which have gone to the making of these English communities through the centuries. It is frightening to find how little these considerations figure in the totalitarian thoroughness of the airport scheme. The very hugeness of the project dwarfs the individual out of existence. If one public house were to be compulsorily closed there would be a public inquiry with KC's to fight for the licensee's rights; if a slum clearance were to be mooted the battle would rage for days with every individual interest involved. But with the airport the first consideration is, "The airport must be developed in stages and the construction of each stage should interfere as little as possible with its use." About the people on the land - nothing.

The feeble protest which the local residents have been able to put up against the steam-roller of a Government Department has gained some grudging consideration. There may be pre-fabs or concrete houses for those driven from their homes which they need not accept if they don't want to. The Ministry of Civil Aviation itself will be the arbiter in the question of accommodation to be given in lieu.

The same Ministry will also decide what compensation it is going to pay and it will take no responsibility for finding alternative sites for churches, shops, farms or businesses. From their decision in the interests of the airport there is no appeal, no impartial arbitration. It is as though a foreign country had conquered the land and were turning out its inhabitants.

Is there no one to stand up to the Government in the interests of these people, peaceable Englishmen, whose only crime is that the land on which they live and work and which their fathers have defended through the centuries is coveted by a Government Department? ..."

Excerpt from *The Middlesex Advertiser and Gazette*, 5 December 1947

therefore have been acquired under the Act. But there was the practical difficulty that the works could not just be closed down; another site would have to be found. Long and ill-tempered negotiations were held with the Middlesex County Council which owned the works but the Council could see no possibility of finding an alternative site without resort to a public inquiry. This the Air Ministry was determined to avoid at all costs as an inquiry would have revealed the true reasons behind the acquisition of the land. Rather than face a public inquiry the Air Ministry revised the layout of the airport which avoided taking the works in the first instance. The frustration felt by the Ministry over the problem can be seen in the letter from the Ministry to the Middlesex County Council dated 1 May 1944 which said:

> *I am directed to inform you that the increasing urgency of the need for an adequate airfield in the London area for the war requirements of the RAF and the inevitable delay which would arise in removal of your Council's sludge works from the Perry Oaks site has made it essential to adopt an amended lay-out which will avoid the immediate necessity for interference with the land in your Council's possession …*
>
> *It is anticipated that the extension of the airfield and consequently the removal of the sludge works will ultimately prove necessary and I am therefore to request that you will be good enough to continue your survey for a suitable site on which the sludge works could be provided and that you will advise the Department as soon as possible of any suitable site your enquiries may be able to find.*

The search for a suitable site continued for the next 50 years and, as described later it was only the presence of the sludge works that prevented the construction of a fifth terminal at Heathrow in the early 1980's. In the intervening years responsibility for the works passed from the Middlesex County Council to the Thames Water Authority and then, when it was privatised, to Thames Water which sold the site to BAA in the late 1990s for the construction of Terminal 5. Cynics will not be at all surprised to learn that the first Chief Executive of Thames Water when it was privatised in 1988 had formerly been a very senior member of the management of British Airways.

The attitude of Winston Churchill: Although the problems of noise and the fate of the unfortunate inhabitants of Heathrow who faced eviction from their homes never even entered the minds of the Air Ministry, a problem that could not be ignored was a minute from the Prime Minister himself addressed to the Secretary of State for Air (Sir Archibald Sinclair) dated 12 February 1944. In this Churchill stated: *'We ought not to withdraw 3000 men for this purpose (the development of the airport) until OVERLORD is over …OVERLORD dominates the scene. I shall suggest to the Cabinet that the project be reconsidered in six months time…'* (OVERLORD was the code name for the Normandy landings).

To the rather lame reply from Sinclair, Churchill retorted, *'I am not convinced. You always ask for everything. No one ever says 'No' to expenditure of men and money.'*

Churchill's attitude caused consternation in the Air Ministry which foresaw that if the project were to be delayed for six months from the Normandy landing the war in Europe could well be over and the reasons given for the development of Heathrow would disappear. Making a virtue of necessity the Air Ministry therefore put forward the revised plan which avoided the Perry Oaks sludge works and Sinclair, in a further minute to Churchill, informed him that *'A new scheme has been prepared, the essence of which is that by re-siting runways it enables us to meet war needs more quickly and with much less manpower during the OVERLORD period.'*

Sinclair failed to reveal that the modified proposals meant, as the Air Ministry well knew, that if they eventually gained subsequent approval for the development of a civil airport one of the runways proposed in the revised plan would have to be demolished. This fact is clear from the reaction of the BOAC which was party to the conspiracy and which bitterly complained about the unsuitability of the revised proposals for their civil aviation requirements. (The runway was built and subsequently abandoned without its ever having been used, because it went through the central terminal area!).

Heathrow Airport under construction, 1945. View from the southwest with the Perry Oaks sludge works in the foreground. The runway going diagonally across the photograph had to be built to keep up the pretence that the airport was needed by the RAF. Its construction was opposed by BOAC because it was entirely unsuitable for civil aviation and it was subsequently abandoned. The writer of a minute, dated 9 January 1946, later made rueful reference to this fact when he said, *'The NW/SE runway constructed by the RAF is completely redundant. That this runway might eventually be redundant to the civil scheme was known when construction commenced. But the period of use of the redundant runway will be less than two years. Its cost will have been approx £350,000'* (equivalent to nearly 10 million pounds at 2007 prices). (Photograph courtesy of the RAF Museum, Reference No. 6082-9.)

In the early part of 1944 Churchill obviously had far more important things to worry about than the development of Heathrow and no doubt this was the reason why he eventually gave his reluctant consent. Following this, approval for the development was given at the meeting of the War Cabinet held on 13 April 1944. The Civil Aviation lobby in the Air Ministry had won and development started in June, the month of the Normandy landings and of the first V1 attacks on London. It shows their blind determination to push ahead at all costs with the project even if it meant diverting valuable resources away from the war effort. This included building the runway that BOAC had opposed and which was subsequently abandoned (see below).

References

1. Balfour, H.H., *Wings Over Westminster.* Hutchinson, London 1973
2. Jay, Douglas. *Change and Fortune: A Political Record.* Longmans, London 1981
3. Buchanan, C. *No Way to the Airport,* Longmans, London 1981
4. MVA Consultancy. *Attitudes to Noise from Aviation Sources in England (ANASE).* Report commissioned by the Department for Transport, London 2007

Chapter Two

The Development of the Airport
1944–1960

Preliminary stages

The Air Ministry's proposals were to construct the airport in three stages. Stage 1 and 2 are shown in the map on page which is dated October 1943. This map shows the runways to be constructed as part of Stage 1 of the development in black. The extensions of the runways which would have occurred in Stage 2 are shaded. The proposals involved the removal of the Perry Oaks sludge disposal works. The difficulty of finding an alternative site for the sludge works without holding a public inquiry led to these proposals being abandoned.

Stage 3 was put forward at the first meeting held, on 10 August 1943, of the Departmental Committee which had been set up to consider the development of Heathrow. At that meeting a completely new plan for the development was proposed. It involved moving the site to the north and centring it on the Bath Road. However it was considered that although this scheme had considerable merits, *'no Government would be prepared to consider a project that involved razing the three old world villages of Harmondsworth, Sipson and Harlington to the ground'* and the matter of a possible Stage 3 development was not pursued at that time. (As will be seen later this rebuff did not put an end to the proposal which was later raised again, gained approval, abandoned and then resurrected 60 years later!).

Work on the construction of Stage 1, as modified to avoid the sludge disposal works at Perry Oaks, began in June 1944. The proposals as approved for Stages 1 and 2 involved the demolition of 117 houses, 8 factories or places of work other than farms and the eviction of 500 people. The schedule of dispossessions for Stage 1 was:

Date	Farm Houses	Dwelling Houses	Cottages
1 June 1944	0	0	2
15 June 1944	3	2	1
1 August 1944	2	2	6
15 September 1944	4	5	16
1 November 1944	3	11	3
2 February 1945	4	3	7
Total	**16**	**23**	**35**

The dispossessions involved the demolition of all buildings south of the Bath Road from Harlington Corner to Longford with the exception of those close to, or facing on to, the Bath Road and those in the Perry Oaks area.

Stage 1 had not been completed when the airport was transferred from the Air Ministry to the Ministry of Civil Aviation (MCA) on 1 January 1946. Despite all the spurious claims about the urgent RAF need, the airport had never been used by the RAF and the first use of the airport was for a civil flight, which took place for publicity purposes, when a British South American Airways Lancastrian took off on a long distance proving flight to South America. The airport was formally opened on 31 May 1946.

Before the transfer of the airport to the MCA a Cabinet Committee on Civil Aviation had been set up. This Committee recommended that the name of the airport should be changed from 'Heathrow' to 'London Airport' on the grounds that 'Heathrow' was difficult for most foreigners to pronounce (thankfully the Committee rejected the fatuous recommendation made earlier that the airport should be re-named, 'St. George's Airport'). The Committee also revised the proposed stages of development; three stages were still envisaged but these differed considerably from the previous proposals. The stages now planned were:

Stage 1. This was to be completed by 31 December 1947 and involved the compulsory purchase of all the land required for the airport south of the Bath Road. This meant the acquisition of 2650 acres of land including the 1590 acres requisitioned by the RAF under the Defence of the Realm Act and the demolition of 215 houses.

Stage 2. This was to be completed by 31 December 1949 and did not involve any further acquisition of land or buildings.

Stage 3. This was to be completed in the period 1950/53 and involved the resurrection of the proposals to extend the airport north of the Bath Road. It included the purchase of 1600 acres of land and the re-housing of the occupants of 950 houses (for presentational reasons the Committee decided to refer to the number of houses rather than the number of people, which was in excess of 3000).

The original proposals also included the demolition of the ancient parish church of Harlington which dates back to the twelfth century and has the finest Norman doorway in Middlesex (see page 118). This raised strong objections from the Diocese of London and the Royal Commission on Historical Monuments. To overcome these objections the absurd suggestion was made that the church should be dismantled stone-by-stone and rebuilt on another site – Twickenham was suggested but it is not clear why. Eventually it was agreed that there was no need to demolish the church and the map shows an enclave on the north-east boundary of the extended airport where the boundary was re-adjusted round the church.

When Stage 3 was announced in 1946 no firm dates were given as to when the extension of the airport to the north of the Bath Road would take place. By 1948 serious delays were occurring with the development of the airport and concern was being expressed about the costs. The date of the extensions was therefore deferred to 1955 at the earliest. A sarcastic editorial in the Middlesex Advertiser and Gazette of 27 August 1948 referred to these delays thus:

What an agreeable and satisfying experience is the planning on paper of a big project. You take a map of an area seven square miles in extent, and having decided to your own satisfaction what are the difficulties to be overcome, you proceed to draw on it runways, taxiways, aprons and so on where the map shows farms, villages and roadways. Then you say, 'presto this shall be an airport' and sit back and expect it to happen. If someone ventures to ask, what about the cost, whence are the labour and materials to come, where are the displaced persons to go, what of the valuable land and resources diverted from essential production, you blandly reply that such considerations are not in your terms of reference.

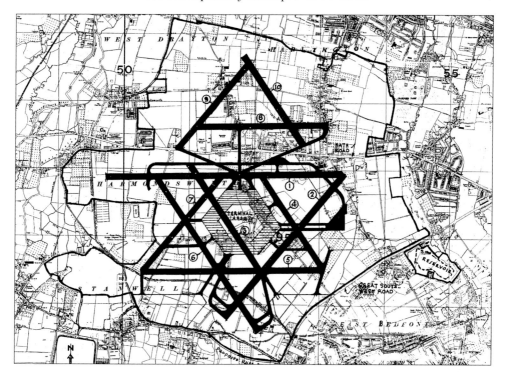

Proposals for the extended airport, 1946 (from TNA file AIR 19/388). The proposals for Stage 3 were agreed by the Cabinet on 10 January 1946 and are shown in the map. They involved the complete destruction of Sipson and the greater part of Harlington. The map shows that the proposed northern boundary approximately follows the line of the M4 motorway which was conceived in 1946 as a replacement for the Bath Road which would have had to be closed.

FRIDAY, OCTOBER 18, 1946   EVENING STANDARD—PAGE

HEATHROW TO SWEEP AWAY 2 VILLAGES

Churches will be demolished
to make room for runways

Evening Standard Heathrow Reporter

LONDON AIRPORT, Friday. — The Middlesex villages of Sipson and Harlington, 14 miles from London, will disappear from the map, and an aircraft runway will cross ground where a hospital now stands, when the Ministry of Civil Aviation start extending London Airport north of the Bath-road in four years' time.

**Headline from the Evening Standard
18 October 1946**

Looking again at the report of the Layout Panel of London Airport one gets the idea that it was conceived in such a fashion. There was an easy optimism about it which assumed that the first stage of the plan was already completed, that the second stage was to be finished in 1949 and the third was to be completed by 1953. That was twenty months ago, and already it is being discovered how little account had been taken of realities. In fact the first stage is still in progress having got little beyond the three runways at Heathrow constructed by the RAF; the second stage, only just begun has run into difficulties because of the capital cuts imposed to regulate the scarce manpower and labour; the third stage cannot get going before 1953 if at all.

A touch of realism is brought to the project by the recent report of the Select Committee called into being when it was seen things were not going according to plan. Yet even in this report there is a frightening disregard of the public who have nothing to do with the Airport except to bear its cost and suffer its inconveniences. The huge runways are spread out over the countryside, flattening villages, eating up farmland and destroying roadways, and for all this loss to themselves the public, by the mad reckoning which passes for political economy in these days, have to foot the bill, so that they have to pay at both ends.

The Select Committee heard no witnesses from the doomed villages of Sipson and Harlington, made no inquiry into the loss of production on the requisitioned lands and no one has attempted to estimate the extra cost imposed on road transport by the proposed diversion of the Bath Road. The Airport as at present planned is a monstrous prodigality...'

Throughout the period 1948–1950 the uncertainty as to when or whether the airport would be extended continued. In October 1950 the Ministry of Civil Aviation announced that it had revised its plans for the airport extension. The revised plan shown above involved a smaller area of land and reprieved parts of Harlington and Sipson. However, Harmondsworth which hitherto had been just outside the threatened area now found itself a potential victim.

The proposals included an extraordinary 'wedge' of land in which houses in Harmondsworth were to remain although cut off from the rest of the village and surrounded by the airport on three sides. The map is also remarkable for the manner in which the proposed boundary of the airport was drawn to exclude residential areas. This was, no doubt, for the best of reasons but the environment of the residents had the extensions been built does not bear thinking about. It shows yet again the total failure of the authorities to have any regard for the amenities of the residents of the Heathrow area which has characterised their attitude from the beginning.

The residents of Harmondsworth now found themselves allied with those of Sipson and Harlington in resisting the development. The resistance compared with the later anti-airport campaigns at Cublington and Stansted was strangely muted. There was undoubted resentment but a curious apathy prevailed, no doubt inherited from the war-time years when people had become conditioned to being directed and told what to do by the authorities. The general feeling seemed to be that if the Ministry had made up its mind nothing could stop it. At a public meeting one view expressed was that, 'it would be un-British to resist a development that the Government had declared was in the public interest' although at the same meeting the Vicar of Harmondsworth declared that, 'although he did not mind having a church without a steeple he would fight any development which meant that he had a church without people.'

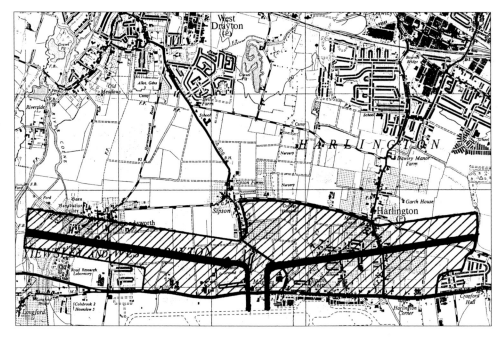

Modified proposals for the extended airport, 1950.

𝕸𝖎𝖉𝖉𝖑𝖊𝖘𝖊𝖝 𝕬𝖉𝖛𝖊𝖗𝖙𝖎𝖘𝖊𝖗 𝖆𝖓𝖉

B   BUCKINGHAMSHIRE ADVERTISER   H/
THE UXBRIDGE GAZETTE   R(
The Old-Established   C(

Vol. CX. No. 5856   **FRIDAY, DECEMBER 19, 195:**

In the slipstream of the Airport news : thousands rejoice and give thanks

'THE MOST WONDERFUL CHRISTMAS BOX WE'VE EVER HAD'

www.icUxbridge.co.uk   Wednesday, December 17, 2003

Runway uncertainty goes on for villagers

Contrasting headlines from the editions of *The Uxbridge Gazette* of 19 December 1952 and of 17 December 2003. The first celebrates the end of the first attempt to construct a third runway at Heathrow. The celebrations were premature; who would then have thought that the aviation industry would have been so persistent in its demands for the expansion of Heathrow that 51 years later almost to the day it would still be pressing for expansion.

Although the effect of the proposals on the threatened area was calamitous the Ministry refused to consider any compensation for owners or occupiers of property in advance of the property being requisitioned. Moreover it declared that compensation would be at pre-war values and would not take account of price rises due to the scarcity of housing in post-war years. As a result only the most urgent repairs were carried out to the houses affected (950 at first, 665 after the proposed stage 3 had been modified). The situation was particularly serious for owner-occupiers who found themselves in a position of being unable to sell when they wanted to move house.

Throughout 1951 and the early part of 1952 the Ministry of Civil Aviation continued with its cat-and-mouse policy of threatening to come north of the Bath Road but refusing to say when, other than that it would not be before 1955. By mid 1952, however, doubts were beginning to be expressed as to whether the airport would ever be extended across to the north side of the Bath Road and in December 1952 the Ministry finally announced that the scheme had been abandoned.

The futility of the years of uncertainty was well summed-up in the editorial of the Middlesex Advertiser and Gazette of 19 December 1952:

For over six years there has been an intermittent controversy regarding the effect of London Airport plans on the communities settled in the land to be occupied. Every now and then there would be a 'final' revision of the plan to add impetus to the controversy. The Government's decision last week (to abandon the plan) makes it plain that the grandiose scheme for the airport as first planned was adopted too easily without due regard to the consequences to the people it was proposed to disturb. Now that the part of the plan for the northern side of the Bath Road has been found to be not needed, all the anxiety and loss which has been the lot of the inhabitants of the threatened area over the past six years is shown to have been unnecessary and it could have been avoided if there had been more consideration and earlier consultation with the people concerned.

The same editorial also has some harsh things to say about public apathy and the lack of support for the resistance groups formed to fight the extension of the airport. Some of these groups, now transformed into residents' and amenity associations, survive and like to think that they were responsible for preventing the development. In fact as the editorial goes on to say:

The case for the inhabitants (and those concerned are in an area far larger than the actual site proposed for the airport) has had far too feeble support from the public. There have been a few valiant fighters but they have lacked the strong public backing sufficient to impress the authorities. The few have stuck to their guns but it would be a mistake to assume that the Government has capitulated to their protestations. The reason for the Government's decision is that the extension of the Airport is no longer considered necessary, and that is some-thing entirely different.

Having been reprieved from destruction the villages around the airport had to endure life with the airport as their neighbour. Forty years later the threat of destruction reared its ugly head, but was suspended again only to be raised yet again 10 years later. How this came about and how the airport has affected the area around Heathrow is considered later in Parts 3 and 4.

The first Control Tower, *c*.1946 (WDLHS). An airport cannot operate without a control tower so this was one of the first buildings to be erected on the airport. It was a crude utilitarian building with direct access from the Bath Road just a short distance to the north. It stood roughly where the airport police station now stands.

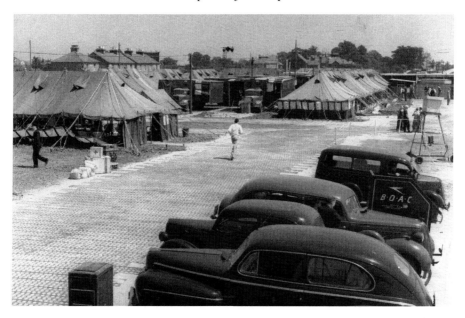

Terminal area, 1946. The first 'terminal' area was this temporary tented accommodation hastily erected on the north side of the airport. There was no clear need for the airport to be brought into use so soon and, until such time as the airport was ready, flights could easily have been made from one of the RAF bases close to London. Indeed RAF Northolt was used by British European Airways for civil flights until 1954. There were others reasonably close to London which would have had much better facilities for passengers and caused them far less inconvenience. However, this would have raised the question as to why one of these bases had not been developed in preference to Heathrow. (Photographs courtesy of BAA plc).

Terminal area, 1946 (K. Pearce). Another view of the tented terminal area, taken from the Bath Road. Until the airport tunnel into the central terminal area was opened this was the main entrance into the airport, then known as 'London Airport North'. In the foreground is the sign board of what was then the 'Bricklayer's Arms' (see below).

The 'Air Hostess'. This public house began life as the 'Bricklayer's Arms'. It replaced a pub of the same name which was demolished in 1928 to allow for the widening of the Bath Road. It stood directly opposite the temporary terminal area (see above) and was re-named in 1954. It was demolished in 1988 and its site is now occupied by a drive-in McDonald's.

'Departure Lounge', and Flight Departure, 1946. These photographs clearly shows the primitive facilities that were available to passengers and the inconvenience to which they were put so as to keep up the pretence that there was an urgent need for an airfield at Heathrow. The top photograph shows the interior of one of the marquees depicted in the previous photograph, the lower photograph shows passengers boarding an aeroplane. (Photographs courtesy of BAA plc).

Terminal buildings, late 1940s (Uxbridge Library). The tents shown in the earlier photograph soon gave way to these pre-fabricated buildings which continued in use until the central terminal area was developed.

Opposite below: **The second control tower, early 1950s** (WDLHS). This was one of the first buildings to be erected in the central terminal area to replace the earlier building shown on page 90. Designed by Frederick Gibbard and architecturally much superior to its crude predecessor it was later designated as a listed building. It has since been succeeded by a new control tower built as part of the Terminal 5 development.

Interior of one of the pre-fabricated huts serving as a terminal (Uxbridge Library)

Exterior of terminal area, 1951 (WDLHS). The facilities offered to passengers in the temporary terminal buildings were so primitive that they came to the attention of the local Public Health Inspectors. This photograph is one of a series showing the disgusting conditions discovered by the PHIs which were used as evidence to bring a prosecution against the airport authorities. A close examination of the area in front of the two oil drums towards the rear reveals the presence of a dead rat! The pair of cottages in the background was situated on the other side of the Bath Road just to the east of its junction with Bolton's Lane.

Control tower

Main access tunnel

Access tunnel to the central terminal area: top, 1955; bottom, 2008. The tunnel was initially constructed to provide access from the Bath Road to the central terminal area. It opened to traffic in 1953 and in 1965 a spur road was opened between the M4 motorway and the entrance to the tunnel. The tunnel originally had two lanes for traffic with provision for pedestrians at a higher level in the remaining lane on each side. The pedestrian access lanes have since been converted for use by traffic.

The Central Terminal Area, 1961. The view is to the east with the control tower just left of centre, immediately behind it is the Queen's Building and to its right is the first terminal building to be built. It was then known as Number 1 Building Europa but is now part of Terminal 2. Terminal 1 was later built on the area of vacant land to the left of the Queen's Building. In the far distance are the BEA maintenance buildings and in between in solitary isolation is the original Fairey hangar. This could not be demolished until the legal dispute with the Fairey Aviation Company over the ownership of the land had been settled.

In the meantime, with the construction of the runways largely completed, attention had to be turned to providing suitable access and terminal facilities. The remaining photographs in this chapter therefore deal with this aspect.

Chapter Three

Ancillary Developments

Introduction

For some years after the decision was made to abandon the proposed development of the airport to the north of the Bath Road all official attention was concentrated on completing the airport to the original plans. This was not surprising as the development had fallen well behind schedule and the escalating costs were a persistent source of concern. In 1953 the decision was taken to develop Gatwick as a second airport for London to take flight diversions from Heathrow during bad weather and at peak flying times.

These developments were obviously enough to be going on with as far as official action was concerned. However, there are two other effects of the creation of a modern airport that are of equal significance to the noise problem. They both result from the ripple effects of siting a landing strip in the middle of a stretch of countryside. The first is the physical effect, not only on the area of the airport itself, but on a huge swath all around it. The second is the economic effect – the creation not just of thousands of new jobs for people dependent on the airport but of a host of other new commercial openings created by those industries which home in on an airport like a moth to a flame.

Hotels and offices

The first of these ancillary effects to become apparent was the demand for off-airport parking followed by a proliferation of hotels on the airport perimeter. The Skyways Hotel on the Bath Road, which opened in 1959, was the first hotel to appear. This was built on the site of Bedford Lodge, a Georgian house which stood in a large garden. It was but the first example of the replacement of an old existing building in sympathy with its surroundings by modern systems-built blocks of no architectural merit. It was followed, in 1961, by the Ariel Hotel (since re-named as the Holiday Inn) built on the site of the 'Coach and Horses', an 18th-century inn needlessly demolished to make way for it. Since then many other hotels too numerous to mention by name have been built mostly on the Bath Road frontage of the airport.

Surface access

Road: In the autumn of 1962 work started on the construction of the M4 motorway with a spur road linking the M4 to the centre of the airport. As described earlier the motorway had originally been conceived as a replacement for the Bath Road and was to have been the northern boundary of the airport. The road opened to traffic in 1965 and has been another significant factor in attracting commercial developments to the Heathrow area.

Coach and Horses, Harlington Corner with the Ariel Hotel (now The Holiday Inn) 1960.
Soon after this photograph was taken the old 18th-century coaching inn was demolished.

Ibis Hotel, Bath Road, Harlington Corner, 2004. This hotel was built in the 1980s on the site of Ash Cottage, a large house which dated from the early 19th century.

The Sheraton Skyline and Marriott Hotels, Bath Road, 2007. Before the airport the north side of the Bath Road between Harlington Corner and Sipson Corner was lined with largish houses intermingled with cottages. These have all disappeared to make way for hotels and offices.

Bath Road Farm, *c.*1900. At the time that this photograph was taken the farmhouse was the only building on the Bath Road between Longford and The Magpies. The photograph shows the author's great-grandfather Thomas Cottrell with his daughter Emma standing outside. The house was demolished in the mid-1970s and replaced with the office block known as Heathrow Boulevard shown below.

Heathrow Boulevard, Bath Road, 1995. This office development was built on the site of Bath Road farm.

From the opening of the M4 with a spur road to Heathrow in 1964 until the completion of the M25 in 1985 little was done to improve road access to the airport. The Greater London Plan of 1944 had envisaged a series of ring roads around the capital and the E-ring road of the plan came to fruition as the M25 Motorway. It was built to link together the other motorways around London and although it is the major motorway link for Heathrow this was the last part to be completed. It had been started in 1975 and the final (Heathrow) section of its 120-miles was formally opened by Margaret Thatcher on 29 October 1986. By then it was already becoming a national joke or a disgrace, depending on whether or not one used it. Although Margaret Thatcher, notorious for lacking any sense either of humour or of proportion, did not see it that way. She boldly declared '*Some people are saying that the road is too small. Even that it is a disaster. I must say that I cannot stand those who carp and criticise when they ought to be congratulating Britain on a magnificent achievement.*'

It had been expected to carry 79,000 vehicles/day by 2001 but within five years it was already carrying more than 200,000 and it is the busiest motorway in the country. From time to time plans have therefore been made to widen it but these have been met with such public hostility that they have always had to be scaled-down. However, as a result of the decision to construct a fifth terminal at Heathrow the motorway has been widened to dual 5 lanes south of the airport spur junction (14), which links the terminal to the M25, and dual 6 lanes between this junction and the junction with the M4 (15).

The route is the national network's most critical strategic point, carrying traffic from the junction with the M3 to the M4 interchange, in addition to thousands of vehicles heading to and from London's main airport and fleets of lorries travelling between the Channel ports, the West Country and south Wales. Its vulnerability to delays is worsened by the fact that 50 per cent of traffic either joins or leaves along the stretch, resulting in a high level of lane-switching. The widening was originally approved by the Conservative government in 1995 but was denounced as 'madness' by John Prescott the opposition transport spokesman and consequently it was shelved within weeks of Labour's election victory in 1997. However, John Prescott who was by then the Deputy Prime Minister later confirmed his madness.

Aerial view of Harlington, 1962. This photograph was taken just before the construction of the M4 motorway was about to begin. Harlington village surrounded by fields on either side is in the middle.

Aerial view of Harlington and Sipson, 1966. Comparison of this and the previous photograph shows the effect that the M4 motorway and airport spur had on the landscape. Harlington is to the right of centre, Sipson is on the extreme left.

The M25 motorway, near Heathrow

Rail: To help relieve road congestion to the airport an extension to the Piccadilly line from Hounslow West to the three terminals in the centre was opened in 1976. It was later extended to include a link to the fourth terminal which made obvious sense. At the same time as this extension was made, an extension to the Perry Oaks site was also partially constructed at the expense of BAA even before any suggestion that a fifth terminal was envisaged for that site! This was done without any publicity and is not widely known but it is characteristic of the long-term plans for the expansion of Heathrow.

The Piccadilly line extension had little adverse environmental effect as the line runs underground for almost its entire length. The line provides direct access to central London with a travelling time of 45 minutes but unfortunately the trains are not suited to the carriage of passengers with a large amount of luggage nor can they be adapted. Proposals were therefore made in 1988 to connect the airport to the British Rail mainline into Paddington which could provide a high-speed non-stop service.

The link to the main line at Hayes was originally to have been above ground, passing over the M4 on a 6-metre high viaduct, and gradually coming down to ground level before going underground to the airport centre. The plan was rejected on environmental grounds and most of the link was eventually built in a tunnel. The delays in choosing the route meant that it did not become operational until 1998. Now completed under the name 'Heathrow Express' it provides a non-stop service from the airport centre to Paddington with a journey time of only 15 minutes. However, the cheapest single fare (in 2007) was £15.50 and at more than £1.00 per mile it is one of the most expensive forms of travel in the world. To meet this criticism a cheaper but slower service known as 'Heathrow Connect' became operational in 2006. This links to the main line at Hayes and stops at all stations between there and Paddington, in 2007 a single fare from the airport to Paddington was £6.90 but the last leg of the journey between Hayes and the airport a prohibitive £4.90.

Hatton Cross Station. This was the first station to be opened on the extension to the Piccadilly line from Hounslow West which was constructed to help relieve road congestion to the airport. The route to the central terminal area was completed in 1976.

Hayes station itself already has a good service to Paddington and it is on the route of the proposed Crossrail project that would link Paddington and Liverpool Street stations by means of a new deep tunnel. If built Crossrail would revolutionise east-west traffic across London and give the capital something similar to that which Paris has had since 1965. The likely cost is between £10 and £15 billion i.e. similar to the cost of the ill-conceived Concorde project but far more useful.

Chapter Four

The Airport's Neighbours

Surrounding the airport are what were once the old villages of West Middlesex – Cranford, Harlington, Sipson, Harmondsworth, Longford, Colnbrook, Poyle, Stanwellmoor, Stanwell, West Bedfont and East Bedfont. All rich in history and architecture which struggle to survive and retain some of their identity. It is an uneven battle and some such as Cranford have already succumbed whilst others, such as Harmondsworth and Stanwell, still appear as oases in an urbanised desert.

In the case of Harlington, Sipson and Harmondsworth a determined attempt has already once been made to completely remove them from the map. Sixty years later this threat has again become a reality with the proposals, described in Chapter 4 of Part 3, to construct a third runway and a sixth terminal which would involve the obliteration of Sipson and make Harlington and Harmondsworth uninhabitable.

Many residents have no choice but to either lodge futile complaints or move and the more affluent residents with no particular ties to the area, either by way of family or work, do of course move out but 'tolerate or emigrate' is not an option for many people. To add insult to injury BAA states that it is environmentally responsible and a good neighbour of the local communities; the newspaper cutting shown opposite typifies its approach. Actions, quite literally in this case, speak louder than words.

Villages under threat

All the villages mentioned so far although inevitably affected by airport-related activities have not actually been threatened with physical destruction. Unfortunately the same is not true of the three villages of Harmondsworth, Harlington and Sipson that lie to the north of the airport between the A4 and the M4. In the past 60 years all three have been threatened on more than one occasion and none more so than Sipson.

Sipson: Sipson is a village in the north-east of the parish of Harmondsworth. It is the second largest settlement in the parish and is first recorded as Sibbeston in a manorial document of 1110. The name is of Anglo-Saxon origin and it must have existed long before it appeared in the records. In the Harmondsworth Parish Registers it frequently appears as Shepiston which has led to the erroneous assumption that the name is derived from the town-ship of sheep. In fact it is said to mean 'Sibwin's tun' which reflects the earlier name and has nothing whatever to do with sheep.

The latest threat to the village came in late 2007 when the Government announced that it fully accepted all the proposals for expansion of Heathrow put forward by the aviation industry and which are described in Part 4. These would involve the complete destruction of the village to make way for the construction of a third runway and a sixth terminal.

GETTING on with the neighbours is critical to the future development of the airport and its image. Tensions are bound to surface with the surrounding community wherever an operation exists on the scale of Heathrow, but Heathrow Airport Ltd (HAL) is keen to see these resolved.

Issues of concern to local residents include noise, congested roads, air quality and safety.

HAL is rightly concerned to ensure it always behaves as a good neighbour.

For over 20 years community links have been strengthened by the existence of Heathrow Airport Consultative Committee.

It was formed to provide an effective forum to 'thrash out' issues regarding the development and operation of Heathrow Airport which have an impact on people living and working in the surrounding areas.

The forum allows interested parties to be

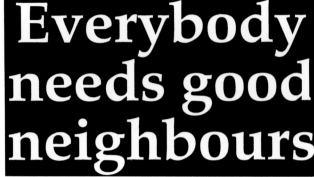

Everybody needs good neighbours

Advertisement placed by BAA in The Heathrow Recorder, December 1992.

a) British Airways is committed to being a good neighbour, concerned for the community and environment. We continually strive to improve our social and environmental performance, with the objective of ensuring that our activities contribute to the sustainable development of the communities in which we operate.

b) British Airways is supporting the development of an additional, short runway at Heathrow. We believe that a third Heathrow runway is consistent with the principles of sustainable development as long as measures are taken to reduce adverse environmental and local impacts

Excerpts from British Airways' Social and Environmental Report for 2002/2003!

The reality, or the neighbour from hell. Aircraft coming in to land over Cranford. Depending on wind direction and which runway is in use overflying can occur for several hours at intervals of little more than two minutes. The only relief for those afflicted is when flights are switched to the other runway.

Church of St Dunstan, Cranford. *'The church lies all on its own and is reached from the village by a drive and across a hump-backed bridge. There is great charm in this solitude.'* So wrote Pevsner in the *Buildings of Middlesex* in 1951. Viewed from the south, as in this photograph, this still seems to be the case but it fails to reveal the presence of the M4 motorway only 100 yards to the north of the church. Nor can it reveal the deafening roar of traffic and aircraft in the once-peaceful churchyard. If a third runway at Heathrow were ever to be built it would end less than one-mile away from the church which would be directly under the flight path.

Stanwell Village (photos G. Smeed). The village is hemmed-in by the airport to the north and by reservoirs to the south-west which paradoxically help it to retain its own separate identity. It is the best-preserved of the airport villages and the top photograph, looking towards the 12th Century church of St Mary is deceptively rural. But the photograph below, taken from the top of the church tower and looking in the other direction, shows all too clearly the influence of the airport.

Church of St Mary, East Bedfont. Bedfont parish was cut in half by the construction of the Great South West Road in the 1930s. Most of it to the north of the road, including much of the hamlet of Hatton, was then destroyed to make way for the airport. However, despite the proximity of the airport and the traffic the central part around the village green and 12th century church still retains some semblance of a village character.

The Ostrich Inn, Colnbrook. Colnbrook, little more than two miles from the end of the main runway, was the lunch-time stop for stage coaches heading west out of London and the final changing point for horses from the west to London. In airline parlance it was an important traffic hub and this is reflected in the many coaching inns which still line its High Street. The Ostrich with its central carriageway to allow carriages into the yard behind, is, unquestionably, the finest of these. It dates from the 12th century but the present building is largely early 16th century.

Longford Village centre. Longford on the Bath Road is on the very edge of the airport with Terminal 5 less than half-mile to the south. It retains its village character largely because the Bath Road was superseded by the Colnbrook by-pass in 1928. Among the many interesting buildings is the timber-framed 'White Horse' dating from the 16th century and which can be seen in the middle distance.

Tour of Sipson village

Sipson is a linear village which straggles for about ¾-mile along Sipson Road from the 'Plough' public house in the north to the junction of Sipson Road with the Bath Road.

On the road from West Drayton, the 'Plough' public house (B on the map) is the first building in the village itself. This is a modest mid-19th-century inn that is now completely overshadowed by what is now the 'Holiday Inn' (A on the map). Planning permission for this monstrosity under its original name of the 'Post House Hotel' was given on appeal in 1969. The next photograph shows that until the early 1960s the 'Plough' stood alone at the northern end of the village and was a prominent feature; although unchanged since then it is now so overwhelmed by the hotel and the garden centre to its south that it could be easily missed.

About 300 yards south of the 'Plough' at the staggered cross-roads in the centre of the village is the 'King William IV', Sipson's second and most interesting public house (D on the map).

It is a late mediaeval Grade II listed building, unusual in style for West Middlesex, and is known as a 'Wealdon' type house because of its prevalence in the Kent area. There are only two such houses within the Borough of Hillingdon and the King William is remarkably fine in that internally one can still appreciate the pattern of an open hall rising through two storeys with accommodation on two floors at each end. The centre has been in-filled, but the building still retains its character and, although re-fronted, its medieval origins are very clear from the side elevations and roof form.

About 150 yards from the King William and along Harmondsworth Lane is a Grade II listed farmhouse (D). It is listed as being late 17th century but is possibly much earlier. Unfortunately it has been rather unsympathetically restored in recent years so that it has lost some of its original charm and character.

Almost opposite the farmhouse is the village school (E). This moved from its original site on the Bath Road in 1966 because of the aircraft noise. Paradoxically its previous name

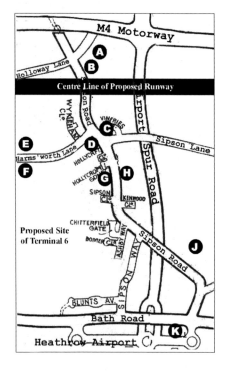

Map of Sipson, 2007. A = Holiday Inn Hotel; B = The 'Plough'; C = Former Baptist Church; D = The 'King William IV'; E = Primary School; F = Old Farmhouse; G = Post Office; H = The 'Crown'; J = Sipson Court; K = Yhe 'Three Magpies'.

Entrance to Sipson Village from Harlington, 2007.

Sipson from the air, 1949. The view is from the north and was taken to illustrate the threat to the village at that time. It shows the village high street still bordered by fields in intensive agricultural production and an area to the east of the village which was to be designated as 'helicopter area'.

'The Plough', Sipson, 2007.

'The King William IV', Sipson, 1982.

Sipson Road, 1952 after a blizzard, as seen on the way from West Drayton. The photograph shows the relative isolation of the village at that time. The 'Plough' was the first building at the extreme north of the village. Ten years later the land in the foreground was carved-up by the construction of the M4 and the realignment of the local roads. Twenty years later the 'Post

House' hotel (now Holiday Inn) was built on the land on the left side of the road. The gateway in the hedgerow is approximately where the entrance to the hotel is located.

of Sipson and Heathrow School was dropped in favour of its present name although the school is unquestionably in Sipson and not Heathrow.

Returning to Sipson Road and at its junction with Sipson Lane is the former Baptist Church (C). This building dates from the early 1900s but as its congregation declined it was converted into residential accommodation now known as Church Court. However, the external appearance has been largely retained.

One hundred yards further south on the left-side of the road is the 'Crown' public house (H) which dates from the mid 19th century. Opposite is the Village Stores and Post Office (G). At first sight this seems to be an undistinguished late 19th-century building but there has been a shop on this site for at least 200 years and much of an original building even older than this lies hidden behind the Victorian front. This back half is half-timbered with low ceilings and could well be the oldest building in Sipson but surprisingly it is not listed.

Just past the Post Office are Holly Cottages dating from 1906 and now re-numbered as 432–450 Sipson Road. Almost opposite is the former Gladstone Terrace of about 1880 and now re-numbered as 415–423. Both were formerly occupied by farm workers employed by Wild and Robbins of Sipson Farm and are shown below.

Everything else in the village street from this point is mostly post-1935 and of lesser interest. The main exception is a pair of modest mid 19th Century cottages now numbered as 499 and 501 Sipson Road opposite the junction of Sipson Road with Sipson Way. Architecturally they are of no interest but their original name 'Scroogeall Cottages' can still be seen on a plaque just under the eaves. This strange name is derived from the name of the field on which they are built and could be the origin of the name of Ebenezer Scrooge given by Charles Dickens to the chief character of *A Christmas Carol*. Dickens is known to have been a frequent visitor to Sipson House which stands nearby and he may have picked up the name of the field on one of his visits.

Opposite Scroogeall Cottages is Sipson Way which with its houses dates from 1923. This provides a short cut from Sipson Road to the Bath Road. Before this the only link with the Bath Road was at Sipson Corner.

On the way to Sipson Corner on the left side of the road is (or to be more precise was) Sipson House (J) an attractive Grade II listed Georgian house standing back from the road. It apparently still substantially survives as office accommodation under its new name of Sipson Court. However, in the 1970s the house was acquired by BAA which failed to maintain it and it became in a ruinous condition.

17th-century farmhouse in 1998 after restoration, Harmondsworth Lane, Sipson.

Heathrow School, Harmondsworth Lane, Sipson, 2005.

Church Court (formerly Sipson Baptist Church), Sipson Lane, Sipson.

Sipson Village Stores and Post Office. The Victorian addition crudely added to a much older medieval building hidden at the back.

Sipson Road, Sipson, looking south.

Sipson Way, Sipson, looking north.

At a point about one hundred yards further south Sipson Road meets the Bath Road. All about is dreary modern development associated with Heathrow Airport but just across the road is the 'Three Magpies' public house a unique survivor of a bygone age (K).

Just south of the 'Three Magpies' is another unique survivor in the form of the barrel of an 18th-century cannon half-buried in the ground. The history of this is described in Chapter 3 of Part 1. It is rather difficult to see because it is on the fringe of the airport and surrounded by busy roads. Just to the left of the 'Three Magpies' is the beginning of a road which is all that remains of Heathrow Road which linked the hamlet of Heathrow with the Bath Road.

If the proposals for the expansion of Heathrow were ever to be implemented everything described above would be buried under concrete. This has been the fate threatened for Sipson ever since 1946. Evidence for this can be seen from the earlier photograph dating from the late 1940s which shows the village high street still bordered by fields in intensive agricultural production and an area to the east of the village designated as 'helicopter area'.

Sipson Court, neo-Georgian office accommodation in Sipson Road. Because of its ruinous condition permission was therefore given by Hillingdon Council for the 'restoration' of Sipson House and its conversion to offices. This 'restoration' took the form of the complete demolition of everything except the front façade so that the present building is little more than a neo-Georgian replica.

The 'Three Magpies', Bath Road. This 18th-century coaching inn, which in 1765 was known as the 'Three Pigeons', has been extensively restored but it is the only survivor of the many such inns that once lined the Bath Road in the vicinity of Heathrow.

Derelict agricultural land of former Sipson Farm. This is Grade I agricultural land but like much of the land around Heathrow it has been neglected to 'enhance' its possible development potential. This land could be growing vegetables currently imported by air from all over the world.

Church of St Peter & St Paul, Harlington. Harlington was first mentioned in an Anglo Saxon land charter of 831 AD and again in the Domesday Survey of 1086. Its church dates from the 12th century and has what is generally considered to be the finest Norman doorway in Middlesex. The village has suffered more than most from its proximity to the airport and most of its historic buildings have disappeared to make way for airport-related developments. The church came under threat when, in 1946, it was proposed to extend the airport up to the line of what is now the M4 motorway and would be made unusable, if not demolished, were a third runway to be constructed.

Harlington Church, as seen from M4 motorway bridge.

Harlington Baptist Church. The Baptists have had a presence in Harlington since 1775 but having outgrown their original building (which still remains) moved to this fine building with its neoclassical façade in 1879. It is the most dominant building in the village High Street and is listed as Grade II.

The Dower House, High Street, Harlington. Apart from the parish church this is probably the oldest building in Harlington. It dates from the 16th century and is timber-framed with a brick-frontage added later in the 18th century.

Harmondsworth Village centre, 1974. The village which is less than ½-mile from the airport's northern perimeter still retains many of its old buildings. The oldest is the 12th-century church of St Mary which has a Norman doorway comparable with that of its neighbour at Harlington, a Tudor brick tower and a pretty cupola typical of the churches of West Middlesex. To the immediate right is the Sun House (formerly 'The Sun' public house) and on the left is the 'Five Bells' both dating from the 16th century. The present-day view is exactly the same except that the police box and air-raid siren have since been removed.

The Great Barn. The Grade 1 listed barn, which is also a scheduled ancient monument, stands just to the west of the church. It dates from about 1450 and according to John Betjeman is the finest mediaeval barn in England. It is certainly one of the largest being 191 ft in length and 38 ft wide and has survived virtually intact since it was first built. Although unique it has been threatened more than once by demolition to make way for an extension of the airport.

View of church and barn – with the shape of things to come? The view of the church and barn is genuine but that of the aircraft about to land is a fake. However, if a third runway were ever to be built this would be the view assuming that the buildings themselves were not demolished – which is by no means certain.

Manor Farm, Harmondsworth. The view is from the church tower and the great barn is just to the right outside the picture. Until the early 1970s this was a working farm and the barn was still in use for agricultural purposes. The farm house has since been converted to office accommodation. It occupies the site of the former manor house; is Grade II listed and dates from the early 19th century. In the background are the offices of British Airways – 'Waterside' – see page 134.

Chapter Five

The Search for Alternative Sites

Gatwick

The Gatwick Race Course Company opened a race course in 1891, complete with its own railway station. In 1930 land alongside the racecourse was purchased for use as a small aerodrome, which was licensed in August 1930 and became known as Gatwick Aerodrome. In 1933 it was purchased by a private company that became Airports Ltd and one year later it received a licence from the Air Ministry to operate as a commercial airport. During the Second World War the airfield was requisitioned by the Air Ministry and used by the RAF. It remained under the control of the Government but from 1946 onwards a small number of charter airlines were allowed to operate civilian flights from Gatwick.

From the late 1940s it became apparent that there was a need in SE England for an alternative to Heathrow that could operate when bad weather or other emergency meant that Heathrow could not be used. Stansted was the first option but after much prevarication and an ominous foretaste of things to come, Gatwick proved to be the favoured choice. Thus in 1954 approval was given for the development of the new Gatwick Airport which was very far removed from the bad weather alternative to Heathrow that had been proposed originally. Instead it was to be the second main civil airport to London and it was officially opened on 9 June 1958

Ever increasing passenger numbers meant that the airport soon outgrew its capacity and work began on enlarging it as early as 1962. The terminal was doubled in size and in 1964 the runway was extended to 8,200 feet to accommodate the growing number of jet aircrafts using Gatwick airport. Work began on a second terminal in 1983 and this opened as Gatwick North Terminal in 1988. It has two runways but the northern runway is used only when the main runway is temporarily non-operational because of maintenance or an accident. However, the runways cannot be used at the same time because of insufficient separation between them. Gatwick is now the busiest single runway airport in the world, the second largest airport in the UK and the sixth busiest international airport in the world.

From the outset there have been demands for the construction of an additional runway at the airport. However, this was blocked, at least temporarily, when in 1979 the then British Airports Authority (now BAA plc) signed a legally binding agreement with West Sussex County Council under which BAA undertook not to construct a second runway at Gatwick before 2019. Nevertheless the consultation exercise conducted by the Government in 2004 (and which is discussed in more detail later) did not altogether rule out the construction of the runway after this date. As a result land at Gatwick has been reserved and safeguarded for the future construction of a second runway at Gatwick, in case new ones proposed for both Heathrow and Stansted could not come to fruition.

Civil Airports in Great Britain
(after Buchanan – ref. 1).

Stansted

Even more than Heathrow the saga of the development of Stansted Airport illustrates the extraordinary tenacity of the aviation industry and the stranglehold that it seems to have on whatever Government Department, at any given time, is responsible for civil aviation. Indeed there is an almost constant revolving door relationship between the two with many examples of civil servants leaving government employ to become consultants to the aviation industry and vice versa.

The saga began during WWII in 1942 when the airfield was developed as a base for the USAF. At the end of the war the Ministry of Civil Aviation took control of the airfield with a view to develop it as an alternative to Heathrow during such time that it was closed due to bad weather or other emergency. As described earlier this idea was abandoned when it was decided that Gatwick airport should be used for this purpose.

In 1956, during the height of the Cold War, the airfield was again given over as a base to the USAF which proceeded to construct a new high-capacity runway. The base never became operational and in 1957 the Americans relinquished the airfield to what by then had become the Ministry of Transport and Civil Aviation. The presence of the runway was to influence further events and from then on the civil servants responsible for the development allowed its presence to colour their views in the face of rational decision making. As a Government Minister was later to remark *'It is quite clear, looking back, that at least from 1953 onwards the assumption was consistently made that Stansted would be the third London Airport.'* So not surprisngly the 1963 report of Inter-departmental Committee on the The Third London Airport made up entirely of civil servants and government appointees, and without any public consultation, recommended Stansted as the third London Airport.

Thus began the long war of attrition between the aviation lobby and the local residents that has continued ever since. From time to time the local opposition have appeared to win their case against further development but the one thing for certain is that their battle if far from over.

Aerial view of Stansted Airport, 2007.

Before the expansion of Stansted could go ahead planning legislation required that a Public Inquiry should take place so an inquiry opened on 6th December 1965 and lasted 31 days. In the case of most major projects an Inspector is carefully chosen who is likely to come up with the 'right' answer. This means that the inquiries are little more than a formality and instances where the decision has gone against Government policy are very rare indeed. However, to everyone's surprise the Planning Inspector found against the development his main conclusion being '*That it would be calamity for the neighbourhood if a major airport were to be based at Stansted. Such a decision could only be justified by national necessity which had not been proved by evidence at this inquiry.*' In all his report assessed the Government's proposals on six counts and rejected them on five.

Undeterred by this unexpected setback the Government rejected the report and announced its decision to go ahead with the expansion. At that time Douglas Jay was the Minister responsible for civil aviation and he is on record as believing that '*the gentlemen in Whitehall really do know best.*' However, by mid-1967 he had been replaced by the more environmentally conscious Anthony Crosland who, in view of the hostility created by the Government's decision, announced that a new independent inquiry into the third London airport would take place. This inquiry was to be headed by Mr. Justice Roskill a judge of the High Court and became known as the Roskill Commission.

The Roskill Commission

The Commission started work in May 1968 and ended in December 1970. The length of time taken was reflected in the scale of the inquiry which made a cost-benefit analysis of various possible sites for the location of an airport somewhere in SE England. As a result of these deliberations the possible sites were narrowed down to four possibilities – Cublington, Thurleigh, Nuthampstead and Foulness (Maplin); significantly Stansted was not even on the short-list. Finally Cublington in Buckinghamshire proved to be the optimal choice of the Commission with the dissenting voice of just one member – Colin Buchanan – who argued in favour of Foulness on the Essex coast.

The choice of Cublington as the site for the third London Airport proved to be very unpopular and the widespread concern happened to coincide with a change of government in 1970. The incoming administration did a U-turn and announced that it was in favour of Foulness island as the site of the new airport. The 'foul' in the name actually derives from the presence there of many birds (fowls) but because of the more obvious meaning the site was re-named as Maplin from the sandbanks of that name that lie off the coast at Foulness.

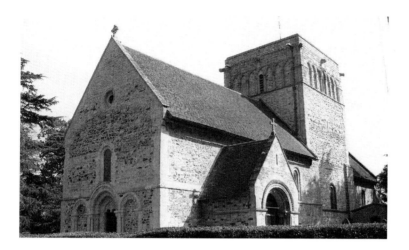

Church of St Michael and All Angels, Stewkley. The Grade I listed church dates from around 1150AD. It is one of only three churches in the country to have escaped extension and modernisation and remains as it was when built – with a few minor internal changes. If an airport had been constructed at Cublington this 12th-century church would have been demolished. Cost-benefit analyses, such as those conducted by the Roskill Commision, cannot put a realistic value on buildings like this. The initial proposal was to value it in terms of its insurance against fire confirming the view that many economists know the price of everything and the value of nothing.

Cublington Spinney. This monument marks the centre of what would have been the airport. The triangular figure is meant to represent a Concorde aircraft in flight. The plaque reads: '*This spinney was planted in 1972 by the Buckinghamshire County Council in gratitude to all those who supported the campaign against the recommendation that London's third airport should be at Cublington. Parish councils, organisation, societies and many individuals contributed towards the costs of the spinney. The point is the centre of the area proposed for the airport. Midmost unmitigated England.*'

Maplin

The announcement by the Government that it intended to develop an airport at Maplin was followed by a consultation document on runway location and alignment which was ready by April 1972. Soon after the Maplin Development Authority was established and in January 1973 the Maplin Development Bill was published to give the necessary powers for work to proceed. The airport would probably have been built but for the fact that in early 1974 a general election was held and a Labour government elected.

The incoming administration was faced with many economic problems not least was the fact that the previous government has been committed to two major projects apart from Maplin. Work on the building of a channel tunnel had already started a year earlier and there was long-standing commitment to proceed with the ill-conceived and ill-fated Concorde project. The latter was a technological folly which subsequently proved to be both an economic and environmental disaster. However, such is the power of the aviation lobby, which never wanted an airport at Maplin in the first place, that the two most useful projects were dropped in favour of proceeding with the development of Concorde. In March 1974 all work on the development of Maplin was suspended and in July the project was officially cancelled. Thus ended the best chance that the country ever had of developing an airport that would satisfy everybody apart from the aviation lobby which has always been in favour of the expansion of Heathrow. Their efforts to this end are discussed in the next chapter and in Part 3.

Other coastal sites

From time to time proposals have been made for the construction of an airport on sandbanks in the Thames estuary. In the late 1980s the Thames Estuary Development Company came forward with a proposal to construct such an airport to be named as 'Marinair' and this possibility was reluctantly considered only to be rejected by the RUCATSE Committee whose deliberations are discussed in Chapter 2 of Part 3. In the early 2000s a site at Cliffe in the Thames estuary was included by the review of possible sites for an airport. However, this

Foulness Island, Essex – another one that got away (J. Savage). If Maplin airport had materialised this would have suffered the same fate as farmland at Heathrow which once looked very similar to this.

Farmland at Stansted – still under threat (P. Riding). An additional runway at Stansted would obliterate this view for ever.

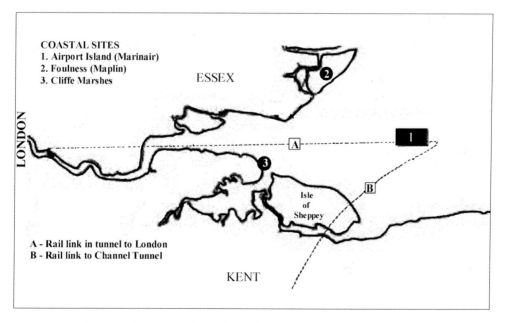

Alternatives - Map showing proposed coastal sites for an airport in the Thames Estuary, complete with rail links to London and mainland Europe.

was widely seen as a feint to allay criticism that the decision to expand Heathrow and Stansted had already been made and predictably the idea was abandoned.

In 2006 a paper by Tony Hall and Peter Hall (4) condemned Heathrow's history as '*a series of minor planning disasters that together make up one of the country's truly great planning catastrophes.*' They considered a number of alternative sites for a new airport and concluded that the case for creating a new island in the Thames Estuary was overwhelmingly strong. It would ensure no aircraft noise over London or the Southeast, no displacement for people currently facing upheaval around London's expanding airports, and direct rail links to mainland Europe, as well as to London and the rest of the UK.

Relocating Heathrow would free up more than 1,000 hectares of land for redevelopment estimated to be worth more than £6.8 billion, with the potential for the creation of a new sustainable community of more than 30,000 homes in one of the country's worst housing hotspots. The authors stressed that the paper was not a plea for the immediate closure of Heathrow – or even for phasing it out in five or ten years' time because '*That would be logistically impossible and economically ruinous. It was a plea for long-term planning that would result in Heathrow's replacement, and eventual closure, over a long period of time: between now and the next century.*'

In January 2009 (5), and following the announcement of the Government's approval of a third runway at Heathrow, Boris Johnson the Mayor of London again raised the possibility of an airport in the Thames estuary as an alternative. He commissioned a study by the engineer responsible for the design of an airport on an artificial island in Hong Kong. This showed that a four runway airport was both technically feasible and would serve Britain better than extending any of the existing London airports. It could be built in 8 years, would cost £40 billion, and would entail splitting the airport in two with runways placed on separate islands linked to each other and to the Essex coast to the north and the Kent coast to the south.

Although all of these proposals have much to commend them it now seemed that the expansion of Heathrow was inevitable.

References

1. Buchanan, Colin. *No Way to the Airport.* Longmans, London 1981
2. Hall, Peter. *Great Planning Disasters.* Weidenfield and Nicholson, London 1981
3. McKie, David. *A sadly mismanaged affair.* Croom Helm, London 1973
4. Hall, Tony and Hall, Peter. *Heathrow – A Retirement Plan.* TCPA, London 2006
5. *Sunday Times* 25 January 2009. Boris unveils £40bn Heathrow-on-Sea

Chapter Six

Back to Heathrow and Developments 1960–1990

The fourth terminal

Up to 1970 the only expansion of the airport, outside the boundaries set in 1952, had been the extension of the northern runway to the west, approval for the construction of which was given in 1967. During the 1960s and early 70s it was becoming apparent that Heathrow and Gatwick as they had been planned would no longer be able to cope with the anticipated expansion of air traffic.

The cancellation in 1974 of the proposal to construct the third London Airport at Foulness (Maplin) increased pressure on Heathrow. Proposals were therefore made, in the mid-1970s, to expand the capacity of Heathrow by constructing a fourth terminal on the southern side of the airport outside its existing perimeter. The Inspector's report of the public inquiry (1), the first ever to have been held over any development at Heathrow, was published in 1979. The result was, of course, a foregone conclusion; in his report the Inspector stated that, *'In my view the present levels of noise around Heathrow are unacceptable in a civilised society'*, but this did not stop him from recommending that permission for the construction of a fourth terminal should be given. This decision in favour of the terminal was taken not because it was the preferred site, but because no other scheme of expansion could be carried out in time to meet the expected demand. The excuse given for the decision was 'overriding national necessity'. However, whilst recommending that approval for the expansion of the airport should be given, the Inspector did go on to say:

> In the past the growth of Heathrow untrammelled by normal planning control has appeared to proceed without proper consideration for its effect on the environment especially in relation to noise. There is an inevitable danger that permission for T4 should be seen by some as yet another instance of precedence being given to the interests of travellers by air over the enjoyment of life by the local population. If this impression is to be dispelled it is, in my view, essential that if they decide to permit T4 the Secretaries of State should re-iterate that it is the Government's policy that there will be neither a fifth terminal nor any other major expansion of Heathrow.

The Government accepted these recommendations and it became official policy that once the fourth terminal was completed no further expansion would be permitted. This was made clear by a statement on 14 February 1980 when Lord Trefgarne the then Government Aviation spokesman in the House of Lords said: '*The Government conclude that the idea of a Fifth Terminal at Heathrow and a second runway at Gatwick should not be pursued. This effectively limits expansion at these airports.*'

An essential requirement of this undertaking was that there would be no increase in the number of aircraft movements (landings and take-offs) beyond a certain figure which the Government announced would be restricted to 275,000 a year. It was also accepted that there should be no increase in night flights.

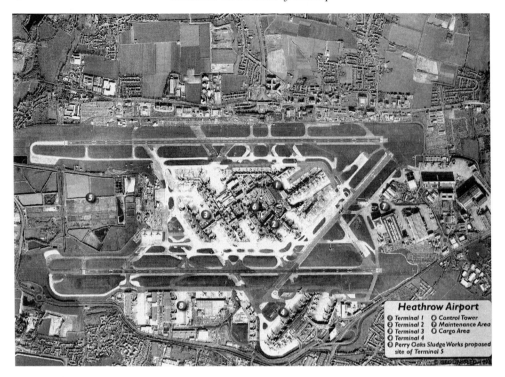

Heathrow Airport from the air, c.1990. The photograph shows the full extent of the airport soon after the fourth terminal had been constructed on the south-eastern edge of the airport. It is remote from the three terminals in the central area and communication between the terminal and the centre is poor. On the western edge between the two main E-W runways is the Perry Oaks sludge works now the site of the fifth terminal. Despite the assurances given at the T4 Inquiry, even before the terminal opened, a determined attempt was made to obtain permission for a fifth terminal. (Photograph courtesy of BAA plc).

    With such unequivocal undertakings from the Government it might reasonably be thought that the matter had been finally decided and, if further airport capacity were needed in the future, it would certainly not be at Heathrow. Within less than three years events were to prove otherwise – as soon as the limit of 275,000 movements a year was reached the restriction was immediately relaxed (by 1991 it had reached 382,000). This was soon followed by a new application to build a fifth terminal, which is described in the next section, and the number of night flights permitted have been steadily increased. Construction of Terminal 4 went ahead and it opened to traffic in 1986. The lay-out of the airport after the Terminal had been constructed is shown in the aerial photograph shown below.

The first attempt at a fifth terminal 1981

The Government's pledge not to expand Heathrow beyond a fourth terminal (which opened to traffic in 1986), coupled with the growth in air traffic, increased the demand for a third London airport which had been shelved by the Maplin review. In the time-scale available it was decided that expansion of Stansted would be the optimum solution because it already had a suitable runway. This was despite the fact that the Roskill Commission had extensively investigated a site for the third airport and had decisively rejected Stansted as unsuitable.

Proposals for the development of Stansted were submitted by BAA in July 1980 but the submission of a counter-proposal meant that the terms of reference of the inquiry into the expansion of Stansted had to be extended to include the possible construction of a fifth terminal at Heathrow. The publicly-owned British Airports Authority (as it then was) affected to be appalled by the counter-proposal and strongly argued against it. The December1982 edition of its newssheet *Airport News* had the headline *'A Fifth Terminal – why BAA says no!'* and a spokesman said: *'Most people assume that airports want to keep expanding regardless of the consequence to others. But as a responsible operator we want to do what is right for air passengers for the industry and the people who live near our airports* (sic).'

Not surprisingly the Stansted resistance groups which had been fighting the expansion of Stansted for the previous 25 years re-mustered their forces to fight yet again. Lobbying against these proposals then began in earnest; the main opponents were (needless to say) the anti-Stansted lobby which had the ungainly acronym NWEEHPA (North West Essex and East Hertfordshire Preservation Association) and British Airways which did not fancy the prospect of having to fly from three airports. British Airways proposed instead that the demand could be met by the construction of a fifth terminal at Heathrow. This was seized on by NWEEHPA which persuaded Uttlesford District Council, the local planning authority for the Stansted area, to submit a planning application for the construction of a fifth terminal at Heathrow on the site of the Perry Oaks sludge works.

The so-called NIMBY (Not In My Back Yard) syndrome is a well-known factor at public inquiries where people naturally wish to protect their own environment. This is understandable and although a protest group is saying, in effect, that the development should go elsewhere most would hesitate before they went so far as to identify a specific alternative site where other people would have to put up with the consequences which they themselves were trying to avoid. This is just what NWEEHPA did by actively campaigning for further development at Heathrow instead of at Stansted. It is almost without precedent among environmental protest movements which with regard to such developments more often adopt the less selfish 'BANANA' approach (Build Absolutely Nothing Anywhere Near Anything).

The application by Uttlesford District Council was supported by British Airways but opposed by the BAA which kept (at least at first) to the Government's policy of restricting the further expansion of Heathrow. The submission of the counter proposal to construct a fifth terminal at Heathrow set the scene for an inquiry that had to be held first at Stansted and then at Heathrow. The first part of the inquiry started at Stansted on 21 September 1981 and ended there after 175 working days on 26 October 1982. It then resumed at Heathrow on 11 January 1983 for a further 83 working days until 5 July 1983.

The Inspector's report (2) in a massive nine volumes was published in 1984. It recommended that Stansted should be expanded and this recommendation was later accepted by the Government. The anti-Stansted campaigners had thus lost the final battle in a war they had been fighting for 25 years during which they had won most of the previous battles. In recommending the expansion of Stansted the Inspector also recommended that:

> *The two applications made by Uttlesford District Council for planning permission for the Extension of Heathrow Airport to provide a new passenger terminal complex and associated facilities and works on land at Heathrow Airport and Perry Oaks Sludge Disposal Works be refused.*

However, the Inspector gratuitously further recommended that:

> *Immediate Government and other action be taken to ensure that the Perry Oaks sludge treatment works is removed and that the site of the works, together with other necessary land to the west of the boundary with the M25, be taken into Heathrow Airport with the object of providing a fifth passenger terminal complex and other airport development with direct access to the motorway as soon as possible.*

Thus in their defeat the anti-Stansted lobby had ensured, without gaining any benefit for themselves, that the possibility of further expansion of Heathrow was kept on the agenda; this despite the strong recommendation, endorsed by the Government, at the T4 inquiry that no such expansion should take place. Graham Eyre, the Inspector at the T5 inquiry, had none of his predecessor's qualms and, in his report, he criticised the T4 inquiry Inspector for making such a recommendation. He went to great lengths to make it clear that the only reason he had recommended that permission for the construction of a fifth terminal should be refused was because:

> *It is unlikely that additional passenger terminal capacity could be constructed, commissioned and in operation at Heathrow in less than a decade from the date of decision to relocate Perry Oaks …Perry Oaks must be moved as expeditiously as possible, it must unquestionably go and its existence cannot reasonably be advanced as a reason for rejecting the expansion of Heathrow beyond four terminals.*

Much of the report of the T5 inquiry reads like a eulogy for civil aviation and the Inspector recommended far more development than even aviation interests had asked for. However, few could disagree with his following statement:

> *The history and development of airports policy on the part of administration after administration of whatever political colour has been characterised by ad hoc expediency, unacceptable and ill-judged procedures, ineptness, vacillation, uncertainty and ill-advised and precipitate judgements. Hopes of a wide sector of the regional population have been frequently raised and dashed. A strong public cynicism has inexorably grown. Political decisions in this field are no longer trusted. The consequences are grave. There will now never be a consensus. Other important policies which do not countenance substantial expansion of airport capacity or new airports have been allowed to develop and have become deeply entrenched. Somewhat paradoxically, such policies are heavily relied upon by thousands of reasonable people who strongly object to airport development. The past performance of Governments guarantees that any decision taken now will provoke criticism and resentment on a wide scale. I do not level this indictment merely as gratuitous criticism nor in order to fan the fires of the long history of controversy but to set the context for current decisions which will shape a future that must enjoy an appropriate measure of certainty and immutability.*

'Prospect Park' – A Trojan Horse?

The acquisition in 1991 by British Airways of some 275 acres of land on Harmondsworth Moor of what it was pleased to call 'Prospect Park' (a name of no geographical or historical significance and merely a figment of BA's imagination) just outside the airport perimeter, potentially represented the first major incursion of the airport into the area north of the Bath Road (A4). Up to this time the airport had been largely kept within its pre-1952 boundaries. There had been exceptions and many of these have had adverse environmental effects. However, in terms of area, as compared with the vast area of the airport, they could not be regarded as significant.

Part of the success in keeping the airport within its existing perimeter had been the policy of the local planning authorities of resisting planning applications connected with airport development. For example Hillingdon Council's draft Unitary Development Plan of 1991 stated: '*All activities directly connected with the airport will be expected to locate within its boundary …Sites outside the airport will not therefore be regarded as available for the expansion of the airport or airport-related activities.*'

British Airways' proposals as finally submitted to Hillingdon Council involved an undertaking on its part of BA to acquire an area of 109 hectares (270 acres) of land bounded on the south by the A4 (Colnbrook by-pass), on the west by the M25 motorway, on the north by the M4 motorway and skirting round Harmondsworth village on the east. In the south-east corner of this site the company proposed to develop 5.3 hectares (13 acres) its Corporate Headquarters and Business Centre which was subsequently re-named 'Waterside'. In return for being given permission to build their office block, British Airways undertook to purchase the remaining 104 hectares of land and to lay this out as public parkland to be known as 'Prospect Park'.

Although this proposal ran counter to Council policy as stated in its Unitary Development Plan, the revised scheme received favourable consideration from Hillingdon Council which, as it happened, owned about half the total 270 acres of the land in question. The official reason for the Council's attitude was that much of the land had been dug for gravel and, as a result of bad restoration, was lying derelict. This rather begged the question of why it had been allowed to become in this condition in the first place. As both landowner and local planning authority, Hillingdon Council and its predecessor authorities were uniquely placed to ensure, when granting permission for gravel extraction, that the land was restored to whatever condition that it liked to impose.

When the revised planning application by British Airways came before the Council for consideration the Council therefore expressed the view that 'it was minded to approve it'. It could not give outright approval but had to refer the matter to the Department of the Environment (DOE) because the development was a major departure from officially recognised policy on the Metropolitan Green Belt. As a result of the referral, the DOE arranged for a Public Inquiry to be held which took place between 26 November and 11 December 1991. At the Inquiry British Airways application was vigorously supported by Hillingdon Council but opposed by neighbouring planning authorities and numerous local and environmental groups.

In his report, which was published in October 1992, the Inspector (3) recommended that British Airways should be given permission to develop the site. He concluded that:

> *There is no policy advice which would justify acceptance of BA's business case as so special as would justify development contrary to the Development Plan and there is no suggestion that BA's future would be put in jeopardy without a Corporate Business Centre at Prospect Park.' But he then went on to say that 'The most important consideration, in my opinion, is whether the environmental improvements leading to the establishment of a major informal recreation resource, open to the public, would justify the sacrifice of a part of the Green Belt.' He concluded that the environmental benefits did outweigh the loss of Green Belt land for the office development and recommended that planning permission should be granted for the development.*

The Inspector dismissed as conjectural the possibility that Prospect Park would be engulfed by a third runway but subsequent events were to show that it was a distinct possibility. At the time, as BA well knew, and which is discussed later the RUCATSE Committee was about to come up with proposals for a third runway that would cut across Prospect Park and leave BA's offices well placed to become a sixth terminal.

Prospect Park was subsequently developed as a pleasant area and it has since reverted to is original name of Harmondsworth Moor. The RUCATSE proposals for a third runway were not pursued at the time but the more recent proposals for a third runway would still devastate the area. This can be seen from the map on page 149 which shows the most recent (2007) proposals for a third runway. It shows that Harmondsworth Moor would be at the very end of the runway and two access roads would be built across it this completely negating any value it might have as a public park.

Above: BA Office site from Colnbrook by-pass 1990; below: BA Offices (Waterside) 1998. The office block was built on an old rubbish tip in the south east corner of the site. Before it could be built this rubbish, some of which is toxic, had to be removed and deposited elsewhere. This was a difficult task and the site seemed a strange choice, if the wish to build its Headquarters Offices had been the only reason why British Airways acquired the land. As already mentioned, the underlying reason may perhaps have been the belief at the time that the office site would be well placed for use as a sixth terminal if a third runway were ever to be built.

References

1. Glidewell, I.D.L. *Report of the Fourth Terminal Inquiry*. HMSO, London 1979
2. Eyre, Graham. *The Airports Inquiries 198–83 (Expansion of Stansted: Fifth Terminal at Heathrow)*. Report in nine volumes – no date or publisher given
3. Department of the Environment. *Prospect Park Appeal decision 12 October 1992*. Reference LRP219/ R5510/02

PART THREE

The Pressures for Further Expansion

Chapter One

The Fifth Terminal

As described in earlier chapters the Perry Oaks sludge works, which occupied an enclave between the two main runways on the western edge of the airport, had long been a thorn in the flesh of the aviation lobby. However, by the early 1990s an alternative site and method of disposal had been found which freed the Perry Oaks site for the construction of a fifth terminal. As a result BAA submitted a planning application for the construction of a terminal on the Perry Oaks site and because of the far-reaching implications of this a Public Inquiry was held into the development.

Apart from the local authorities around Heathrow, opposed to the development, many environmental groups and resident's associations also registered as objectors and appeared at the Inquiry to give evidence and cross-examine BAA and its allies. The progress of the T5 development had already slipped by one year by the time that the first pre-inquiry meeting was held in May 1994. At that meeting the Inspector stated that he anticipated that the main inquiry would start in May 1995 and that it would go on for at least 18 months (i.e. late 1996). This proved to be wildly optimistic as the unexpectedly large number of organisations opposed to BAA, the degree of expertise on which they could draw, and the incredible commitment of some of the environmental groups, meant that the Inquiry lasted far longer than anticipated. BAA had assumed that the Inquiry would begin in 1994 and end in 1995 and in the normal course of events this would not have been an unreasonable assumption. At most public inquiries a developer faces only one major antagonist but for each Topic of the T5 Inquiry BAA never faced fewer than four. The large number of people presenting evidence and the time taken-up in cross-examination was not foreseen even by BAA's opponents and in the event the Inquiry lasted into 1999.

BAA had proposed that the fifth terminal should be built in stages. It hoped that the first phase would open in 2002 and that it would provide for 10 million passengers a year. The final phase, which BAA intended should be completed by 2016, would bring the total capacity of the terminal to 30 million passengers a year. Instead, because of the strength and ferocity of the opposing groups, the Inquiry had lasted nearly four years – the longest such inquiry ever to be held.

At the beginning of the Inquiry BAA went to great lengths to emphasise that the construction of a fifth terminal would not involve a subsequent demand for a third runway. Mike Roberts the then Managing Director of Heathrow Airport Ltd. went so far as to write a personal letter to every household in the immediate area in which he said 'No airport can be invisible and inaudible. But we aim to live in harmony with our neighbours and the proposals for Terminal 5 will be designed to minimize the impact on local communities. *In particular I would like to assure you that they will NOT require another runway or an increase in night flights*' (his emphasis).

This letter was accompanied by advertisement in the local press designed to allay the fears that the construction of the terminal would be accompanied by future demands for additional runway capacity. Examples of two of these are shown below.

Planning permission for the construction of the terminal was granted in 2001 by which time construction work had already started in anticipation of the result. In his report (1) the Inspector stated that 'he agreed with BAA that the evidence placed before me demonstrates that a third main runway at Heathrow would have such severe and widespread impacts on the environment as to be totally unacceptable. However, I place only limited reliance on BAA's request that the Secretary of State should rule out the prospect of an additional runway'. He then went on to recommend that Terminal 5 should be permitted subject to strict conditions. These in particular were:

- that the number of aircraft movements should be limited to 480,000 ATM's a year,
- the area enclosed by the 16-hour 57 dB(A) L_{eq} contour be restricted to 145 km,
- it should be assumed that no further major development would take place at Heathrow after Terminal 5 and,
- Terminal 5 itself should be accepted only if it was substantially subject to the controls set out.

At every public inquiry into proposals for extending Heathrow BAA has claimed that it would not seek any further development. This claim has proved to be false on every single occasion. During the Fifth Terminal Inquiry, as can be seen from the headlines of two editions of its news-sheet, it continually reiterated that it did not wish for a third runway. The edition of 13 January 1999 claimed that '*We don't want to build a third runway at Heathrow and Terminal 5 will not lead to a third runway. But some people simply don't accept this and have caused confusion and worry by claiming that we have a hidden agenda. Well we haven't and we are very concerned to put people's minds at rest on this issue.*' BAA's attitude was later criticised by a Parliamentary Committee on aviation which considered that '*At best the company was culpably short-sighted when it told the Terminal 5 inquiry that an extra runway at Heathrow would be unacceptable for environmental reasons; at worst it was wilfully misleading.*'

Demonstrators against the T5 development. Above: on the opening of the Inquiry on the first day 16 May 1995; below: on the last day in March 1999. Around 18,000 individuals and organisations sent written representations to the Inquiry Secretariat, of which 94% were opposed to the development. The opposition was also reflected in the local public sessions of the Inquiry at which members of the public were given the chance to express their views. At these sessions 290 people came forward of whom 243 (84%) spoke against T5. The crude home-made banners of the protest groups which can be seen in the photographs were in stark contrast to the glossy material of BAA. However, what these groups lacked in funds they made up in commitment.

Artist's impression of Terminal 5 and its link with the M25. The link with the M25 is to be by a completely new spur road which according to BAA will be 'sensitively landscaped and blend seamlessly with the Colne Valley (sic).' The view is highly idealised and in reality it is all too likely that the land around the roads will assume the appearance of so much land around the airport with its car parks, breakers' yards etc. (Illustration courtesy of BAA plc.)

Artist's impression of the main T5 building. (BAA plc.)

Distant view of Terminal 5, 2008. The photograph was taken from Harmondsworth Lane which links Sipson with Harmondsworth. If current plans for a third runway came to fruition all the farmland in the photograph would be taken over and the houses in the distance would become uninhabitable even if they were not scheduled for demolition.

Anti-airport protestors demonstrating against any further expansion on the opening day of T5. The demostration although successful in itself was compelely overshadowed by the ensuing chaos arising from the appalling failure of British Airways to plan the opening day and live up to all its pre-opening hype.

Somewhat surprisingly the Terminal was completed on time and within budget and it was formally opened by the Queen in mid-March 2008. The first flights began on 27 March when it opened fully for business. Prior to its opening British Airways were promising that:

> *At London Heathrow Terminal 5 we've created a natural, logical journey that's so calm, you'll flow through. It shouldn't take long to get from Check-in to Departures. Transferring and arriving are just as simple and calm. Spend the time you save enjoying the excellent range of shops, cafes and restaurants. Or simply relax and be wowed by the world class architecture.*

Never could a company have been more wrong as in reality the opening day proved to be a public relations disaster described by one newspaper as a 'Terminal Disgrace' and another as the biggest public relations disaster since the White Star Line had claimed the Titanic to be unsinkable. By the late afternoon most short-haul flights had been cancelled, the baggage system had failed completely and the terminal was packed with angry passengers. Those lucky enough to reclaim their baggage were faced with long delays whilst the less fortunate had to abandon their baggage completely. Prospective passengers whose flights had been cancelled went home but where this was not possible many had to seek overnight accommodation in local hotels or in extreme cases on the floor of the terminal.

The chaos continued throughout the first week during which 450 flights had to be cancelled and 28,000 items of luggage were mislaid. To add to the misery, 10 days after the opening and just as BA were beginning to overcome their problems, the computer system crashed which meant that all baggage had to be sorted manually. BA had intended to transfer all of their flights to the new terminal but because of continuing problems were unable to do so for another six months. The fiasco over the opening and the resulting bad publicity was estimated to have cost BA £50m.

Reference

1. Vandermeer, Roy. *The Heathrow Terminal Five and Associated Public Inquiries.* Report published in 2001

Chapter Two

Increasing Demands for a Third Main Runway

Following the decision taken in 1952 to abandon the extension of the airport north of the Bath Road (see Part 2) no further proposals were made for additional runway capacity until 1987 when the Chairman of the Airport Transport User's Committee (ATUC) in his Annual Press Conference in 1987 (1) declared:

> *We do not want to ride roughshod over the interests of those living around airports. Equally we do not accept that they should ride roughshod over the interests of millions who want or need to travel whether on holiday or business. . . . To meet the burgeoning demand for both passengers and cargo users it is surely possible to construct an additional commuter runway at Heathrow between the M4 and A4 or a second runway at Gatwick to the south of the present one.*

Such a proposal if implemented at Heathrow would have inevitably meant the total destruction of the villages of Sipson, Harmondsworth and possibly Harlington, and would bring about a massive increase in the number of people severely disturbed by aircraft noise. Presumably the Chairman of the ATUC did not regard this as riding roughshod over the interests of those living near the airport. When he spoke of the interests of those who want to travel on holiday he failed to recognise that social and personal tranquillity require various restraints on the free market. The further expansion of Heathrow would undoubtedly increase demand for air travel, but if through a shortage imposed by considerations of nuisance air travel from Heathrow became more expensive travellers would soon find alternative forms of transport or fly from less fashionable airports.

Although the ATUC is an official body, the proposals were seen as merely the personal opinion of the Chairman and not one to be seriously considered. However, in 1988 the Department of Transport asked the Civil Aviation Authority (CAA) for advice on the adequacy of UK airport capacity in the longer term, taking into account runway, terminal and airspace considerations. In July 1990, following consultations, the CAA reported that by 2005 another runway's capacity would be needed to serve the expected growth of air travel originating in the South East. It identified a number of airports in and near the south east which had potential for further development but advised that, from the standpoint of the interests of users of air services, the preferred locations for new capacity were Gatwick, Heathrow and Stansted. On publication of the CAA report the Department of Transport decided in November 1990 to set up a Working Group on Runway Capacity to Serve the South East (RUCATSE). This Group had responsibility to:

- Evaluate the wider implications of developing additional runway capacity at the sites identified by the CAA.
- Have regard to the considerations, including the environmental considerations, which led the Government in 1985 to the view that second runways should not be built at

either Gatwick or Stansted; and to the relevance of those considerations at Heathrow and at other airports.

•   Test the CAA's conclusions on the contribution of regional airports and to gauge the extent to which these airports can play a part in meeting the overall demand into the next century.

In its initial deliberations RUCATSE drew up a short list of sites which it considered had the most potential for development. It dismissed the possibility that regional airports might play a significant role in alleviating the demand in the south east. In reaching this decision it ignored the fact that a person wishing to travel from say, Manchester to New Zealand, has first to travel to London and stay overnight in an airport hotel so that he can catch the flight from Heathrow. Because the traveller spent the night before the flight in the South East such a journey is regarded as having originated in the South East.

The RUCATSE Committee also initially refused to consider the possibility of constructing a completely new airport (to be called Marinair) in the Thames Estuary which had been proposed by a consortium of developers. It would have been built on the sandbanks some seven miles off Sheerness. The advantages claimed were that it would be privately financed; it would be well positioned for Europe and the Channel Tunnel; it would eventually take more traffic than Heathrow does now; it would disturb no houses, no sleep and no people. These advantages led RUCATSE to concede that Marinair ought to be considered along with other proposals.

The Committee also acknowledged that, apart from the demolitions that were envisaged, the extra noise generated by a third runway at Heathrow would disturb 10 times as many

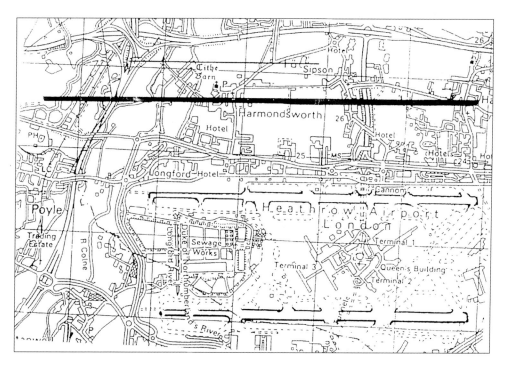

Position of a long third runway as considered by the RUCATSE Committee. The map shows the site proposed for the possible construction of a third main runway at Heathrow. It follows the alignment of the three lanes – Cranford Lane, Sipson Lane and Harmondsworth Lane – which link the villages and ends up by going through the very centre of Harmondsworth Village (Figure 43). The proposal would have taken the airport boundary up to the M4 in the north, the M25 in the west and the River Crane in the east.

people as any of the other options and double the number of people adversely affected by noise from Heathrow. However, this did not deter it from the further pursuit of Heathrow as a strong contender for the construction of an additional runway and in its final report (2) it recommended Heathrow as being the preferred option for an additional runway in the south-east.

Two options were put forward in the RUCATSE report – one being a runway, much the same length as the two existing main runways, which would involve the total destruction of the villages of Harmondsworth, Sipson and Harlington. The other option was for a shorter runway which would spare Harlington from destruction but would inflict a high level of environmental damage on the village. The Committee did not flinch from giving its own estimates of the effects which are summarised in the Table below.

The disappearance of the villages would have meant that some 10,000 people would have to be evicted from their homes. It would also have meant that all the hotels and other commercial development along the Bath Road frontage and elsewhere in the affected area would have been demolished. Although the loss of the hotels might not be mourned, the demolition of the 44 listed buildings identified as being at risk would be an entirely different matter. These include the Grade 1 listed 12th-century Parish Churches of Harlington and Harmondsworth and the 15th-century Great Barn of Harmondsworth which is one of the finest medieval barns in England (page 118).

Apart from the extensive demolition involved the construction of a third runway would also mean a huge increase in the number of people affected by aircraft noise. Communities to the east and west at present hardly affected by noise would at a stroke find themselves on a flight path.

The figures in the Table are so alarming that it might be thought that the mere act of setting them out in this manner should have been sufficient to deter the RUCATSE Committee from

---

EFFECTS OF A THIRD RUNWAY
(RUCATSE Report 1993)

Demolitions:

Houses	3300
Listed buildings	44
Public Buildings	11
Hotels	10
Other commercial	15000
	(m2 floorspace)

Landtake for enlargement (hectares):

Area of existing airport	1197
Area of enlarged airport	1862
Total landtake	665
Green Belt	602
of which:	
Grade 1 Land	427
Other agricultural	22
Recreational	59

Additional landtake for relocations 1500ha. (6 square miles)

Acquisition/relocation costs   **£1162m (1992 prices)**

Total construction costs   **£3271m**

considering Heathrow as the preferred site of an extra runway in the South East. The proposal when taken into consideration with the consequent calamitous effects was so preposterous that few people at first took it seriously and initially it did not therefore meet with the resistance that might have been expected. However, events, described later, were soon to prove otherwise although at the time the Government rejected the RUCATSE recommendations whilst acknowledging that a site for a third runway would have to be found somewhere in the south-east.

References

1. Cox, J.E. *Chairman's Introductory Speech*. Air Transport User's Committee Annual Press Conference 10 December 1987.
2. RUCATSE (Runway Capacity to Serve the South-East). *A report by the Working Group*. Department of Transport, London 1987.

Chapter Three

The Pressures Continue

Although the Government of the day rejected the RUCATSE proposals the Department for Transport (DfT) continued with consultations as to how the expected demand for air travel could be met. It therefore commissioned a study by a company known as Oxford Economic Forecasting (OEF) of the economic benefits of aviation. Despite its name this is a commercial organisation that has no links of any kind with Oxford University and the aviation industry undertook to pay 90% of the costs of the study. As Brendan Sewill (1) has remarked the consultants knew which side their bread was buttered and there was little surprise when the report (2) extolled the economic benefits of the industry. Nor was it surprising when the Department for Transport accepted the report in its entirety and used it as the basis for preparing its own report on the future of aviation in the UK (3).

This report was allegedly a consultation paper and there was a large response to it by various environmental groups. This included the Royal Commission on Environmental Pollution (4) a committee of leading scientists which was specifically set up by Royal Command in 1970 to advise the Government on such matters. However, such is the grip that the aviation industry has on the Department for Transport, all environmental considerations were completely ignored.

Taken at their face value the forecasts depicted in the graph show that by 2030 demand would be growing at the rate of a new Gatwick every 18 months or a new Heathrow every 3 years. Despite the absurdity of these predictions the DfT published a series of consultation papers in 2003 which outlined several options. One of these was a 'short' 2000 metre runway at Heathrow to run between the A4 and the M4 parallel to the two existing E-W runways. This would certainly be welcomed by sections of the aviation industry.

Following the consultation exercises the Government published its White Paper on 'The Future of Air Transport' (5) in December 2003. This made it abundantly clear that the consultation exercise was a complete sham and that the decision to expand Heathrow had been made well before the exercise had even begun. All the public protests had been in vain but the aviation industry was thwarted, at least temporarily, by an unexpected obstacle. For the first time ever they had to be told 'you can't have it now', although if it behaved itself it might eventually gain its wish.

The reason why the Government was unable to comply immediately with the aviation industry's demands was due entirely to the fact that the Government was bound by law to comply with the mandatory air quality limit values for nitrogen oxides laid down by a European Union Directive on air quality that would come into force in 2010. The Heathrow area already exceeded these limits and estimates showed that the construction of a third runway would mean that 35,000 people would be exposed to nitrogen oxide concentrations above the legal limit. The Government therefore had to concede that it could only support the construction of a third runway at Heathrow if the key conditions relating to compliance with air quality limits can be met.

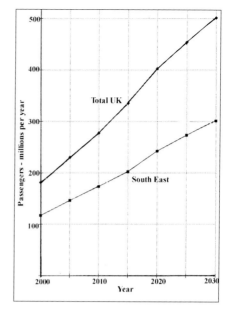

Projected growth in air travel 2000–2030. The Government arrived at its estimates by projecting into the next 30 years the growth encountered in the previous 30 years and this showed that air travel would triple between 2000 and 2030. A forecast is simply that and it does not follow that infrastructure should be provided to meet the expected growth (predict and provide), still less should it be regarded as a target to be achieved.

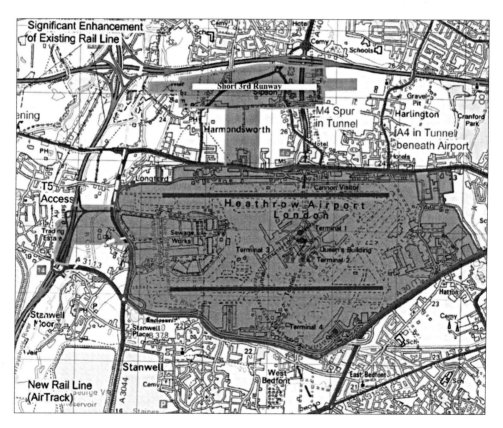

Position of a possible third runway at Heathrow. The grey area represents the extent of the expanded airport with the new runway linked to the existing airport leaving what was left of Harmondsworth and Sipson to be sandwiched between the runways. Because of this the consultation paper claimed that 'only' 260 houses needed to be demolished although it did accept that the historic centre of Harmondsworth village, including the Church and Great Barn, could not survive (from reference 5).

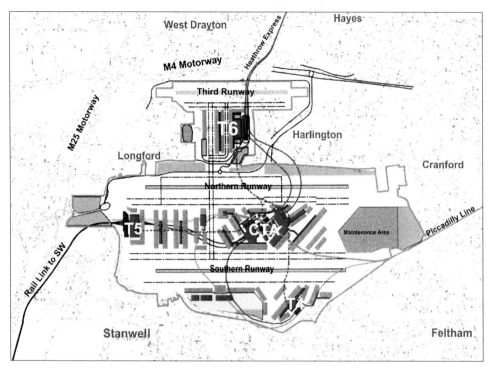

One of a series of proposals produced by BAA for a third runway at Heathrow with an additional terminal (T6). This was produced in 2003 only four years after BAA had repeatedly claimed at the fifth terminal inquiry that *'We don't want to build a third runway at Heathrow and Terminal 5 will not lead to a third runway* (based on map in reference 6).

It estimated that although there was no immediate prospect of this there was a substantially better prospect of achieving the construction of a third runway if it were delayed until 2015–2020. In the meantime it set up a group named 'Project Heathrow' to examine how the problems mainly of air pollution but also noise could be solved. This and subsequent developments are discussed in the next chapter.

BAA, which was on record as being totally opposed to a third runway (see Chapter 2 of Part 3), and earlier had claimed that it did not want a fifth terminal, quickly seized the opportunity and presented plans (6) to include an additional terminal between the existing northern runway and the new 'short' runway to cater for the additional traffic movements. These proposals are shown on the map reproduced above.

References

1. Sewill, Brendan. *The Hidden Cost of Flying.* Aviation Environment Federation, London 2003.

2. OEF. *The Contribution of the Aviation Industry to the UK Economy.* Oxford Economic Forecasting, Oxford 1999.

3. DETR. *The Future of Aviation – The Government's Consultation Document on Air Transport Policy.* Department of the Environment Transport and the Regions, London 2000.

4. RCEP. *The Environmental Effects of Civil Aircraft in Flight.* Royal Commission on Environmental Pollution, London 2002.

5. DfT. *The Future Development of Air Transport in the United Kingdom: South East.* Department for Transport, London 2003.

6. BAA. *Heathrow Airport Interim Master Plan. Draft for consultation.* BAA Heathrow, June 2005.

Chapter Four

The Final Solution?

Project Heathrow

The White Paper 'The Future of Air Transport' of 2003 made clear that the Government supported a short third runway at Heathrow – after a second runway at Stansted – subject to compliance with strict conditions on air quality, noise and public transport access. It claimed that there was a good case for the further development of Heathrow. The airport was said to be of vital importance to the UK economy, attracting business to London and the South East and supporting 100,000 jobs (direct and indirect). A short third runway was alleged to yield net economic benefits of some £6 billion (net present value) – the largest of all the new runway options examined in the run up to the White Paper.

However, it acknowledged the fact that expansion would have environmental consequences and claimed that further development would be conditional on:

- compliance with air quality standards, including EU limits for Nitrogen Dioxide that become mandatory from 2010;
- no net increase in the total area of the 57dBA noise contour compared with summer 2002 – an area of 127 sq. km; and
- improvements in public transport access to the airport (especially rail) and other measures to help reduce the pressures on the surrounding road network.

Notably absent from any of the discussions was any consideration of the social costs of any further expansion and of its effects on local residents who might lose their homes.

To examine how the aims of the White Paper could be fulfilled the work was to be undertaken by a body known as the 'Project for the Sustainable Development of Heathrow' or 'Project Heathrow' for short. This had the terms of reference to:

institute immediately with the airport operator and relevant bodies and agencies a programme of action to consider how the environmental conditions could be met in such a way as to make the most of Heathrow's two existing runways and to enable the addition of a third runway as soon as practicable after a new runway at Stansted.

By using the Freedom of Information Act Justine Greening, a local MP, discovered that the DfT had passed data, which it had withheld from the public, to the airport operator BAA. The information that came to light was revealed by her to the Sunday Times in its edition of 9th March 2008. From this it transpired that the data presented to BAA by the DfT showed that a third runway at Heathrow would immediately breach European noise and pollution limits, ensuring that it could never be built.

BAA and the DfT then worked together to re-engineer the figures to fit the limits. BAA was asked to look at how much quieter (i.e. less noisy) and less polluting planes might become in the future. Together they then kept on altering the predictions of the noise and air pollution from these non-existing aircraft until the could claim that the targets could be met. The meetings between DfT officials and BAA were apparently held on BAA premises and the minutes written-up on BAA notepaper!

The Sunday Times article also revealed the extent to which the aviation mafia had infiltrated into the highest levels of government quoting as examples how the spokesman for Tony Blair when Prime Minister had since found employment as an advisor to BAA and a former junior minsister, now a member of the House of Lords, acted as the spokesman for the Future Heathrow project.

The final results of the deliberations were published under the title 'Adding Capacity at Heathrow Airport' (1) and were unbelievable in going far beyond anything previously considered as remotely possible. Not surprisingly given that all the data had been doctored it claimed that all the environmental conditions set out above could be met even though it envisaged that the capacity of the airport would be effectively doubled by 2020. Among the more improbable were:

Revealed: the plot to expand Heathrow

The paper went on to reveal that unpublished documents obtained under freedom of information laws showed:

– BAA gave instructions to DfT officials on how to "strip out" data that indicated key environmental targets would be breached by the airport.
– The airports operator repeatedly selected alternative data used for the consultation to ensure that the final results showed a negligible impact on noise and pollution.
– The DfT gave BAA unprecedented access to confidential papers and allowed the company to help to rewrite the consultation document.
– The final document significantly reduced the likely carbon emissions caused by the runway by not including incoming international flights.
– An official who was involved in "Project Heathrow" - the DfT unit that researched the environmental impact of the runway was quoted in the newspaper as saying that "It was a classic case of reverse engineering. They knew exactly what results they wanted and fixed the inputs to get there. It's appalling."

The Sunday Times, 9 March 2008

- The claim that noise levels would be lower with over 700,000 planes in 2020 than they were in 2002 with fewer than 470,000 planes a year because planes would be much quieter despite the fact that the next generation of allegedly significantly quieter planes has not yet been designed,
- The claim that only 27 homes would experience air pollution levels above the EU legal limits with mixed-mode in place in 2015 (and 540,000 flights using the airport each year) and that, only 5 years later, with a 3rd runway operational and an increase in flight numbers to over 700,000, there would be be no exceedences!

It would seem that the aviation industry has only to argue that black is white and it expects people to believe it. These claims and other environmental factors are considered in more detail in the next chapter.

Having conveniently dismissed the environmental problems the paper accepted all the proposals in the BAA Masterplan for the airport but then went on to recommend even more wide-ranging developments. Among these were:

- that runway alternation on the two existing runways should be abolished and both should operate in mixed-mode i.e. take offs and landings on the same runway. This could be achieved very quickly and significantly increase the capacity of the airport,
- that the proposed 'short' runway of 2000 metres, mentioned in previous proposals, should be extended by 200 metres and,
- to accommodate this, and possible later extensions of the runway, the existing airport spur road from the M4 should be re-routed further east and placed in a tunnel.

The proposals for the new layout of the airport as envisaged in the report are shown in the map below.

Under the proposals outlined above the village of Sipson would disappear completely whilst most of Harmondsworth and Harlington would become uninhabitable. The DfT claims that 'only' 700 houses would be demolished but the estimate of 3000 in the RUCATSE report (see page 142) is a much more realistic figure. The expansion would take place on land which forms part of the Metropolitan Green Belt. If it came to fruition it would have the effect of removing the whole of the area south of the M4 and east of the M25 motorways from its present Green Belt designation. Most of this area is, of course, open land at present; it would not be in the Green Belt if it were not. This open land would be developed and all the buildings which lie within it would have to be demolished.

All the residential houses, and most of the commercial property, demolished to make way for the expansion would have to be re-located nearby. The only possible location for these would be on Green Belt land outside the area taken up by the expanded airport. Apart from the demolition of existing buildings and their re-location elsewhere, the airport if expanded to the extent which is proposed would lead to extra demand for new development. Even if no additional development took place, the overall effect would be equivalent to the construction of a New Town to

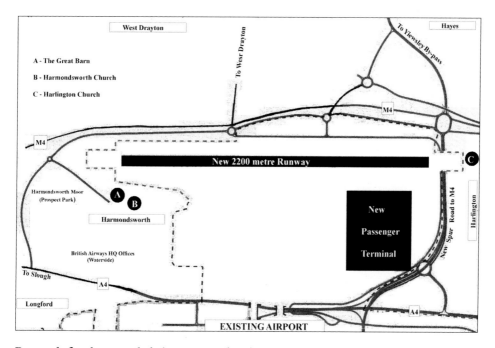

Proposals for the extended airport, 2007 (based on map in reference 1).

accommodate at least 10,000 people, many large hotels, several factories and warehouses of vary-ing size and all the supporting infrastructure that these would require. There would therefore be an enormous loss, on an unprecedented scale, of Green Belt land which would mean that the built-up area of the western suburbs of London would extend, without a break, as far as Slough.

Having set out its proposals they embarked on a Consultation Exercise (2) in which people living in a wide area around Heathrow. Nowhere was the simple question asked as to whether or not respondents wished to see the expansion of Heathrow. To simplify matters the 2M con-sortium of local authorities (so named because it initially represented 2 million residents which have since risen to 4 million) prepared a post paid card with a simple 'yes' or 'no' answer. In all the DfT received a total of 70,000 responses of which 89% were opposed to any expansion.

The Government took some considerable time in replying to the consultation and delayed its response on two occasions. Eventually the decision was announced in Parliament by the Secretary of State for Transport – Geoff Hoon on 15 January 2009. As had been anticipated the decision was to give the green light to BAA for it to go ahead with its plans for the construc-tion of a third runway and a sixth terminal. The government's proposals differed little from this previously put forward. In summary the Government:

- confirmed its support for a third runway, slightly longer (2200m instead of 2000m) and a sixth terminal, Initially subject to a limit of 605,000 air traffic movements which would be subject to review in 2020;
- rejected the introduction of mixed-mode (taking off and landing on both runways) as an interim measure before a third runway became operational;
- confirmed its commitments on noise and air quality and claimed that no additional flights would be allowed from the third runway until it was satisfied that these limits could be met.

Furthermore the Government also claimed that although a third runway could be built:

- additional flights would only be permitted if the EU limits on air pollution and its own limits on noise were not breached;
- the number of planes using the new runway would be limited to 125,000/year rather than then 220,000 originally envisaged to allow the Climate Committee to assess the carbon dioxide emissions. Only if the Committee were satisfied that the emissions would not be excessive and that cleaner planes would come into use would BAA be permitted to go up to 222,000.

These conditions were widely seen as nonsensical and reminiscent of previous pledges on limits set only to be lifted as soon as these limits were reached. Moreover critics asked if it was

Photomontage showing position of runway on existing landscape. In the immediate foreground is the junction of the M4 with the airport spur road which goes off to the left. Under the current (2009) proposals the runway would go over the spur road which would be re-routed about half-mile to the east.

Harmondsworth Lane looking west, 2007. The road, which lies between and is parallel with the Bath Road (A4) and the M4 links Sipson with Harmondsworth. It occupies the approximate line of the proposed runway.

at all likely that BAA would construct a third runway if, in the event, it could not be used to anything like its full capacity.

Further doubt was cast on the Government's claims by research by the impartial House of Commons Library, published less than one month after the announcement and which refuted the Government's environmental and economic case for expansion (3). For example, the Transport Secretary stated that only low emission planes would be allowed to use the new runway. But the House of Commons researchers found that:

> *aircraft designs do not at the moment incorporate many of the features highlighted by the secretary of state' and adds 'unless there are some very rapid improvements in technology, it will be some time before more environmentally friendly commercial aircraft are in widespread operation.*

The research paper also queried the Department of Transport's estimate of £8.2 billion worth of benefits to the economy over 70 years and concluded that it did not account for various factors that could slash the benefits to £1.5 billion or less.

Predictably the proposals were welcomed by the various sections of the aviation industry as they left the way open for BAA to draw up its plans for the expansion and submit them for planning approval at a formal inquiry which would have to be held before final approval could be given. Elsewhere they met with universal condemnation. It was pointed out that every previous approval for the expansion of Heathrow had been subject to certain conditions being met and yet in every single instance once these conditions had been reached they were immediately relaxed. Apart from the enormity of what was being proposed the so-called operational restrictions imposed therefore lacked any credibility.

Crucially the plans were condemned not only by all the organisations that would be expected to do so but also by both of the main opposition parties. In her response to the January 2009 announcement, the Conservative Shadow Transport Secretary, Theresa Villiers, said:

> *Let us be in no doubt: this is a bleak day for our environment and for all those of us who care about safeguarding it. Labour's plans for a third runway at Heathrow would inflict devastating damage on the environment and on quality of life, and the Conservatives will fight them every step of the way.*

In a later interview David Cameron, the Leader of the Opposition, reaffirmed his party's commitment to scrap the third runway should they come to power. He said:

What business needs to recognise is that the third runway is just not going to happen. There is such a coalition of forces against it. There's such an environmental case against.

He also said he did not believe an incoming Conservative government would need to pay compensation since little financial outlay would have been made on the new runway by the next election by BAA.

The Liberal Democrats were equally scathing in their criticism and made a commitment that they would also scrap the runway: Their spokesman claimed that:

the decision to proceed with the third runway is the worst environmental decision that the Government has made in 11 years. It drives a jumbo jet through their Climate Change Act 2008, on which the ink is barely dry. With a commitment to a reduction of 80 per cent in carbon emissions, how can the Secretary of State and his colleagues possibly justify the construction of a new runway? It is also one of the worst political decisions in 11 years it has huge opposition within the Labour party, and has united the opposition in the House and in the country and destroyed the Government's green credentials.

The situation was well summarised by the Chairman of HACAN one of the leading environmental groups opposed to the expansion who said:

A Prime Minister who is showering billions of pounds on the banks is willing to give the go-ahead to a third runway at Heathrow, which may just bring in a little over £1 billion over 70 years. This is the economics of the madhouse.

You have to wonder how long Government Ministers can keep ignoring everything put in front of them. The Environment Agency, Sustainable Development Commission, 2M Group of local authorities, the Mayor of London, the Greater London Assembly, the Liberal Democrats, the Conservative Party and just about every environmental group of any note has told Gordon Brown that Heathrow expansion should not go ahead.

With a general election due in less than 16 months and with the number of hurdles that BAA would have to jump before a planning application could be submitted there was no possibility that this could be done before an election that was widely predicted to lead to a change of government. The matter is considered further in the last chapter of this section.

References

1. DfT. *Adding Capacity at Heathrow Airport*. Department for Transport, London, November 2007.
2. DfT. *Adding Capacity at Heathrow Airport – Consultation Document: Find out more and register your views* . Department for Transport, London 2007.
3. Ares E., Barclay C., Butcher L. and Mellows-Facer A. *Expansion of Heathrow Airport*. House of Commons Research Paper 09/11, February 2009.

Chapter Five

The Hidden Costs

Introduction

The arguments in favour of the expansion of the airport were based on the study by Oxford Economic Forecasting that is discussed in Part 3, Chapter 3. This study was funded by the aviation industry and was accepted in its entirety without question by the industry's acolytes in the Department for Transport. Not surprisingly the various bodies opposed to the developments have challenged whether the economic benefits claimed for the uncontrolled expansion of aviation stand up to critical examination and have attempted to bring the environmental and social costs into the equation. This chapter considers all of these subjects in more detail.

The economic benefits – real or imagined?

Much is made of the importance of the aviation industry to the UK economy and the large number of people it employs either directly or indirectly. Obviously the industry would say that but is it really true?

There are many industries that are far more important but they do not enjoy the many benefits that are given to the aviation industry. Principal among these is the fact that airlines pay no tax on fuel and no VAT is levied on any aspect of air travel. Writing in 2003, Sewill (1) pointed out that, at that time, motorists were paying about 75 pence/litre for fuel whereas airlines were paying only 18 pence. By late 2007 these prices had risen to 100 pence and 26 pence respectively and the proportional difference will remain the same until the tax concession is removed. These figures distort chosen methods of travel so that it is, for example, cheaper to fly from London to Prague than it is to travel from London to Bristol by train.

Sewill concluded (2) that the tax concessions mean that, in effect, £9.2 billion a year in tax subsidies is given to the aviation industry. This figure has been widely quoted and significantly has not been challenged by the industry itself. A number of national environmental groups asked the DfT to re-run its computer model on the assumption that by 2030 air travel would be paying the same rate of tax as car travel. The results showed (2) that:

- demand would rise by 315 million passengers/year instead of 500 million,
- aviation would grow at 2% a year instead of 4%,
- there would be no need for any new runways in the UK, and
- the economic benefit of building new runways would be negative.

Aviation and tourism: The histogram on the next page shows that most of the expected growth in air travel will be due to leisure travel which by 2020 is projected to account for 40% of all air travel. Much is made of these unquestioned benefits to the tourist industry and the assumed benefits to the UK economy. However, in reality there is a net drain on the UK economy caused by the fact that more British residents fly on overseas holidays than there are overseas visitors flying to Britain to take their holidays in this country. The graphs on the next page show how the gap between outgoing and incoming tourist travel is likely to continue.

The graph on the next page shows how the gap between outgoing and incoming tourist travel has widened in recent years and this trend is likely to continue. The figures (from 'Travel Trends 2007' published by the Office for National Statistics) show that UK residents took 70 million overseas flights in 2007 more than double the number of incoming foreign visitors (32 million). The net impact on the UK trade balance was a deficit of £19 billion. Ten years ago (1996) the UK trade deficit on international air travel was just £2.3bn but it has grown dramatically since then as the number of overseas trips by UK residents has more than doubled while the number of foreign tourists visiting the UK has increased at a much slower rate.

Leisure flights are the main driver of growth and fewer than one in seven overseas trips by UK residents is now for business purposes. In 2007 tourists visiting the UK spent at least £18 billion pounds less per year than UK tourists spent going on holiday overseas. Hence expanding aviation simply means increasing the trade deficit for UK tourism.

Apart from this 35% of people travelling to Heathrow are interchange passengers – they never leave the airport. They may be travelling from, say, the USA to India and find it more convenient or cheaper to change flights at Heathrow. The industry claims that if the airport is not expanded these passengers would divert to continental airports such as Paris or Amsterdam. However, they contribute little to the UK economy outside of the aviation industry and it would not be disastrous if they did prefer to switch flights in continental Europe.

Air pollution and global warming

Introduction: Transport by road and air has grown at an ever-increasing pace over the last 100 years and to meet this growth the Department for Transport (DfT) has during this time adopted a policy known as 'Predict and Provide'. In essence this means that predictions are made of the anticipated growth in the particular form of transport, based on a study of past trends, and then provision of the transport infrastructure has been provided to meet this predicted growth. This policy has been criticised partly because it is to some extent self-fulfilling – the predicted growth becomes a target to be achieved and the traffic expands to fill the capacity provided.

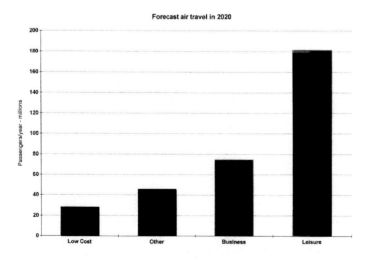

Predicted trends in air travel (DfT). The histogram shows that, if present trends continue, more than 50% of travellers leaving Britain by air would be flying for leisure purposes by 2020.

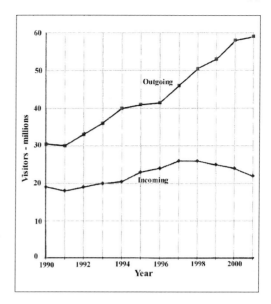

Trends in tourist numbers.
This graph shows the gap
between outgoing and
incoming tourist travel in
recent years..

However, a much more serious criticism is that in recent years it has become increasingly obvious that the predicted growth cannot go on forever because in the long-term it is simply not sustainable. Thus in its report on 'Transport and the Environment' (3) the Royal Commission on Environmental Pollution (RCEP) stated that:

> *An unquestioning attitude towards future growth in air travel and an acceptance that the projected demand for additional facilities and services must be met, are incompatible with the aim of sustainable development.*

The RCEP has reiterated its concern particularly with regard to carbon dioxide emissions from aviation and their contribution to climate change in a more recent report (4).

The DfT has largely abandoned its policy of predict and provide with regard to road building because of criticism and claims to have done so with regard to the provision of airport capacity. However, the RCEP (4) among others, disputes this claim and the recent policy documents published by the DfT show that this is clearly not the case whatever it might say to the contrary.

A consultation paper issued by the Department (5) claims that emissions of carbon dioxide and other, even more harmful, gases will be greatly reduced by improvements in engine technology. Although this may well be so many of these improvements are as yet unproven and it cannot be claimed that a problem is solved by merely pointing to all the efforts made to do so. In any case as the RCEP has pointed out any possible reductions in emissions from individual aircraft are likely to be more than cancelled out by the huge increase in numbers. The amount of carbon dioxide emitted by the combustion of any particular fuel of known chemical composition can be accurately calculated. As this is a basic fact of chemistry there is no possible method of reducing emissions other than by reducing the amount of fuel consumed.

The aviation industry makes much of the fact aviation accounts for less than two per cent of global emissions of carbon dioxide and six per cent of total UK carbon emissions but these statistics are highly misleading. The vast majority of the world's population never travels by air and is never likely to do so and most of the 2% of global emissions comes from Western Europe and North America. Also the figure of 6% quoted for the UK takes no account of the fact that, uniquely, the aircraft emit carbon dioxide at high altitudes where it has an increased effect. It is generally accepted that this figure need to be multiplied by a factor of more than two to account for this increase. This means that in reality aviation already accounts for some 15% of UK greenhouse gas emissions. Nor is it the only factor to be taken into account because the official figures relate only to aircraft leaving the country. Most people leaving or coming to the UK are on return tickets but the emissions from flights into the country are ignored. With the projected increase in air travel it has been reliably estimated that by 2050 aviation would account for at least 40% of UK greenhouse gas emissions if no action is taken to curb air travel.

The increasing concentration of greenhouse gases in the atmosphere is a very serious problem with possible catastrophic consequences. This fact is recognised by the Government which in early 2003 issued a White Paper on energy. The White Paper is supposed to commit the Government to a 'low-carbon' economy in which carbon dioxide emissions would be cut by 60% over the next 50 years. During the same week that the white paper was published the Department for Transport saw fit to re-issue the airport consultation papers predicting a three-fold increase in air travel over a shorter period! If these predictions were realised the amount of carbon dioxide emitted by the aviation industry would at least double even allowing for improvements in fuel economy. If the aviation industry and road transport is allowed to expand and the White Paper is to be taken seriously it will therefore inevitably mean that the other sources of carbon dioxide emission will have to reduce their contribution to carbon dioxide emissions not by 60% but by a far larger amount! The immediate question is why should they?

Before the industrial revolution the concentration of carbon dioxide in the atmosphere was 278 parts per million (ppm) it is now approaching 400 ppm and rising. This dramatic increase in carbon dioxide in the atmosphere is the most likely cause of global warming and it would be incredibly foolish not to act accordingly. However, it would seem that the aviation industry is solely concerned to increase its profits and doesn't worry about a possible environmental catastrophe in the years to come. The Royal Commission on Environmental Pollution (3) defines sustainable development as *'Development that meets the needs of the present without compromising the ability of future generations to meet their own needs.'*

Nitrogen oxides: When hydrocarbons are burnt at 100% efficiency carbon dioxide and water are the only combustion products arising from the fuel itself. However, an internal combustion engine does not burn fuel at 100% efficiency and inevitably small amount of partially-burnt fuel products and nitrogen oxides are also produced which are highly toxic even in small concentrations. The amount of these can be reduced, but not completely eliminated, by the fitting of catalytic converters. This is expected to make a significant reduction in the problem but improvements in engine technology are being overtaken by the growth in traffic so that the reduction may be less than predicted. However, the nitrogen oxides emitted from an internal combustion engine arise from the oxidation of the nitrogen in the air at the high prevailing temperatures and they do not come from the fuel. Flashes of lightening during thunderstorms produce the same effect and changes in the fuel or other improvements if engine technology would therefore have little effect.

Nitrogen oxides are particularly toxic and the EU has set a maximum limit of 40 micrograms (ug) per cubic metre of air that will become mandatory across Europe from 2010. In 2002 a large area around Heathrow Airport already exceed this limit and it was for this reason that at that time the Government could not proceed with the construction of a third runway which if built would have exposed 35,000 people to toxic emissions of nitrogen oxides.

The current consultation document (5) makes the implausible claim that by the time that a third runway was fully operational, in about 2020, improvements in engine technology would be such that the residents of only 17 houses would be exposed to harmful levels of nitrogen oxides! This ludicrously optimistic figure should be compared with the figure of 10,000 people who it was estimated (in 2002) would be exposed to harmful levels by 2015 even if no third runway were built. A report published in 2006 (6) commented that 'All predictions to date showing that air pollution at an expanded Heathrow airport could be successfully mitigated rely on assumptions ranging from the optimistic to the implausible. Further powerful evidence for this came from the report of the Government's very own Environment Agency which in its comments on the proposals (7) stated:

After full consideration of the documents our conclusion is that overall, we do not think that the evidence presented is sufficiently robust to conclude that the proposed Heathrow development will not infringe the (EU) NO2 Directive, bearing in mind the uncertainties that need to be addressed. This is because the assessment of air quality pays insufficient attention to these uncertainties and to the range of possible future scenarios for issues like road traffic, meteorological variability, climate change, background air quality and atmospheric chemistry.

The decision to grant permission to expand based on confidence in an assumption that emission limits will not be exceeded will unquestionably be subject to legal challenge first to the High Court and if that fails to the European Commission. As a sign of things to come, the head of the UK Environment Agency cast doubt over the viability of a third runway at Heathrow and said the government's go-ahead for the expansion of Heathrow defied logic. He was reported as saying that there was a very big chance the runway would never be built and that ministers had made a mistake. In his view the opposing forces would make it difficult for BAA to proceed with extensive planning and design work and he expressed doubt as to whether aircraft engines would become cleaner as rapidly as the government forecasts. The comments may prove significant as the Environment Agency could block the development if ground-level pollution or noise limits at Heathrow were to be breached.

The social costs

Notably missing from any discussions of the proposal to expand Heathrow airport is the effect that this would have on the local community. This callous disregard for the welfare of those affected by the airport has been a factor ever since the idea of an airport at Heathrow was first mooted in 1943 and which was discussed in Chapter 1 of Part 2.

In the present instance the consultation papers estimate that the village of Sipson would be obliterated and that 700 homes would be demolished. However, this refers only to buildings that would be physically destroyed and in fact the villages of Harlington and Harmondsworth would become uninhabitable. The total number of homes affected was estimated, more realistically, by the RUCATSE report (see Chapter 2 of Part 3) to be 3000 and the number of people at least 10,000.

But whatever the figure it is not just a question of the number of houses and people affected – new houses can be built and the people re-accommodated. It is a question of the destruction of whole established communities with their social support systems of shops, pubs, schools, churches and inter-family connections. These factors never seem to be given the slightest consideration but they are vitally important to the people who live in the communities affected. Nothing like the scale of the evictions has been seen since the Highland evictions and those accompanying the enclosures of the 18th century As Oliver Goldsmith remarked of these in his poem the Deserted Village – 'Ill fares the land to hast'ning ills a prey where wealth accumulates and men decay'.

References

1. Sewill, Brendon. *The Hidden Cost of Flying.* Aviation Environment Federation, London 2003.
2. Sewill, Brendon. *Fly Now Grieve Later.* Aviation Environment Federation, London 2005.
3. Royal Commission on Environmental Pollution. *Transport and the Environment.* HMSO, London 1994.
4. Royal Commission on Environmental Pollution. *The Environmental Effects of Civil Aircraft in Flight.* RCEP, London 2002.
5. DfT. *Adding Capacity at Heathrow Airport.* Department for Transport, London 2007.
6. Johnson, T. ad Lockley, P. *Emissions Impossible – An assessment of noise and air pollution problems at Heathrow airport and the measures proposed to tackle them.* Aviation Environment Federation, London 2006.
7. Environment Agency. *Response to the Department of Transport's Consultation Paper 'Adding Capacity at Heathrow Airport'.* Environment Agency Thames Region, November 2007.

Chapter Six

The Last Battle

The events that occurred in 2010 proved to be a turning point in the long battle waged by the various parts of the civil aviation lobby to construct a third E-W runway at Heathrow. As the New Year dawned BAA and its allies were quietly confident that during the year they would be able to submit a planning application for the development with the full support of the Government. As discussed earlier the then Government had not only doctored the figures to justify a third runway but had also proposed a dramatic change in planning procedures that would have made it easier for the construction of a third runway to go ahead. BAA was so confident of success that even before final approval was granted it was talking of further expansion beyond that currently planned. For example in a presentation to the Greater London Assembly by the Chief Executive of BAA he was quoted as saying that 'it would be inappropriate for me to speculate on whether there will be a further case for capacity expansion beyond 2030'. British Airways claimed that a short E-W runway would suffice until 2030 after which further capacity would be required.

These remarks left little doubt that if a third short runway had ever been built it would have been quickly followed by demands that it should be made as long as the other two. With this in place it would then have been an easy matter to extend the existing cross runway to give a four-runway airport. The map below shows how easy it is to anticipate their ultimate aim which had been the hidden agenda of aviation interests for the past sixty years.

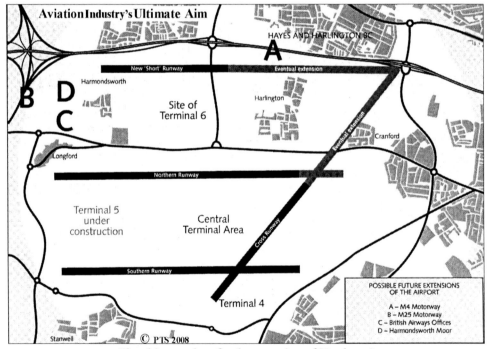

The ultimate plans for the extension of Heathrow?

As might be expected the planned expansion of Heathrow provoked outrage among local inhabitants, local authorities and environmental groups which had learned much from previous campaigns against airport expansion. In the past they had even squabbled among themselves as had happened when the opponents of the expansion of Stansted sought the further expansion of Heathrow as an alternative. However, this time they presented a united front, were well-funded and very well-informed. As a result they combined together to seek a Judicial Review against the Labour Government's decision in January 2009 to give

BAA the green light to draw up detailed plans for a third runway. They scored a notable success in March 2010 when the High Court judge ruled in their favour by declaring that the case for expansion was fundamentally flawed and costs were awarded against the Government. The 2003 White Paper was declared null and void and the case for expansion was effectively killed off, at least for the medium term, by the judge who ruled that it was no longer relevant because it did not take account of the Government's latest policy on climate change or adequately incorporate the new cost of carbon emissions. His ruling meant therefore that before any expansion could possibly take place the Government would have to make a complete re-assessment of the case for expansion in the light of changes that had occurred since 2003. This in itself would have set back any prospects of a third runway by many years but even worse news for the expansionists was soon to follow.

Jubilant campaigners emerging from the Royal Courts of Justice in March 2010. Those present included Susan Kramer (Liberal Democrat for Richmond), John McDonnell (Labour MP for Hayes & Harlington), Justine Greening (Conservative MP for Putney), Ray Puddifoot (Leader of Hillingdon Council), John Stewart (HACAN) and Geraldine Nicholson (NOTRAG). (Photo Courtesy of Greenpeace)

BAA and its allies refused to concede defeat with the Government Minister for aviation and an ardent supporter of the Heathrow expansion going so far as to say that he welcomed the decision. Notwithstanding this set back, the Labour Government continued with its expansion policy and went into the May 2010 election with the expansion of Heathrow in its manifesto.

However, after the High Court judgement the case for a third runway had been on life support and even this was turned off when, in May 2010, the incoming coalition Government announced that it had scrapped plans for a third runway at Heathrow. After nearly a decade of campaigning those opposed to expansion at Heathrow had scored a famous victory. It was a third runway at Heathrow that the aviation industry had wanted above all else but from the outset it was clear that the new coalition Government was to develop a very different policy to the one of expansion pursued by Labour. This was exemplified by the publication in early 2011 of a new consultation paper (1) the preamble to which read:

When this Coalition set out its programme for government last May, we promised great change and real progress. In aviation, we began straight away by cancelling the third runway at Heathrow and making clear our opposition to additional runways at Gatwick and Stansted. The Dft Business Plan makes promoting sustainable aviation one of our five structural reform priorities, with a specific objective to adopt a sustainable framework for aviation in the UK by 2013. There is an urgent need for a genuinely sustainable framework to guide the aviation industry in planning its investment and technological development in the short, medium and long term. The previous government's 2003 White Paper, The Future of Air Transport, is fundamentally out of date, because it fails to give sufficient weight to the challenge of climate change. In maintaining its support for new runways - in particular at Heathrow - in the face of the local environment impacts and mounting evidence of aviation's growing contribution towards climate change, the previous Government got the balance wrong. It failed to adapt its policies to the fact that climate change has become one the gravest threats we face.

This damning verdict on the previous Government's policy and the 2003 White Paper coupled with the previously mentioned verdict of the High Court should, once and for all, effectively kill the case for any further expansion. Hitherto the aviation lobby had won every previous battle but it had lost the last one and that is the one that counts! Even so from past experience it is clear that the aviation industry never gives up and it is virtually certain that at some future date it will seek to re-open the debate; in fact BAA has said that it will do so. However, what is equally certain is that it will never succeed because of the environmental consequences and the strength of the opposition to the scheme. After more than 60 years of a war of attrition the scheme can confidently finally be laid to rest.

Cover page of Hillingdon Council's newsletter celebrating the victory. The photo shows the land across which the runway would have been built with a sixth terminal in the area behind the hedgerow. Sipson village lies off to the left of the photo.

The manner in which the opposition organised their activities and the events that led to their ultimate victory are well summarised in a book by John Stewart, a leading opponent of airport expansion entitled *Victory Against all the Odds.* (2)

An unforeseen consequence, well-described by Robert Chesshyre in an article in the *Independent*, of the long battle against the expansion of Heathrow has been the effect it has had on the village of Sipson. (3) For many years the village was threatened with destruction and householders were unable to sell their homes. In a well-meaning, but ultimately self-defeating, move to help the local MP fought hard to require BAA to buy houses at the full market price from those who wished to move away in advance of the forthcoming destruction. Unfortunately those who departed were families with good jobs and those with the deepest roots in the community.

References

1. DfT. *Developing a Sustainable Framework for UK Aviation: Scoping Document.* Department for Transport (2011). (Downloadable from DfT web page).

2. Stewart John. *Victory Against all the Odds: The story of how the campaign to stop a third runway at Heathrow was won.* HACAN. 2010 (Downloadable from HACAN web page)

3. Chesshyre Robert. 'The Village Paying a Painful Price for Runway Success'. *Independent*, 7 April 2011.